Everyt
Wanted
Galleris
Afraid t

Andrea Bellini

jrp|ringier

The publication has received
generous support
from Nationale Suisse

ART AND ART DEALERS

Art has existed since the dawn of humankind, and works of art have been bought and sold as early as Upper Paleolithic times. The means of circulation of what we might generally refer to as "artefacts" has historically depended on the economic, political, and cultural organization of the societies concerned. From prehistory to historic times, artworks were acquired through barter until the first coins were minted in the seventh century AD. Roman aristocrats often purchased Hellenistic sculptures, and, in the Middle Ages, artists and studios sold their works directly to the Church, to the aristocracy, and to the upper-middle classes. It was the rapid expansion of the middle class that, between the seventeenth and nineteenth centuries, gradually encouraged the development of a new art market.

No longer dependent on religious, aristocratic, and political patrons, who had imposed their own subjects and content, artists enjoyed a creative freedom that led to the work of the historic avant-garde movements. But this new situation necessitated an intermediary between artists and their new potential patrons. Thus emerged, as early as the nineteenth century, the figure of the art dealer as we know it today.

From the outset, this was more than just another profession. Those who took it up were eclectic, cultured, and eccentric personalities, and in many cases, they made an essential contribution to the knowledge and circulation of the art of their period. Paul Durand-Ruel, the first real art dealer of the modern age, provides a fine example. Born in 1831, the young French gallery owner had, by age thirty-one, adopted an innovative approach to the trading practices of his day. Durand-Ruel represented his artists exclusively, promoting their work through solo exhibitions and an international network of galleries, which provided the public free access to the exhibition premises. He ultimately established a close alliance between the art market and the world of finance. Thanks to Durand-Ruel, Impressionism soon enjoyed widespread fame and considerable economic success.

Daniel-Henry Kahnweiler, a German art dealer whose career was much inspired by that of Durand-Ruel, played a similar role for Cubism. In 1907, at the age of just twenty-three, Kahnweiler opened his first gallery in Paris. He supported his artists financially and promoted them through a wide network of activities, an approach that became characteristic of the finest gallery owners of the twentieth century. He visited his artists every day, discussing their work and progress with them; he photographed and archived all their works; and he brought their work to new audiences through his remarkable operations as a publisher.

Thus, in the early twentieth century, long before museums and other institutions took up this role, private galleries were becoming places of intellectual interaction and artistic experimentation. Arguably, the entire history of twentieth-century art unfolded in these galleries, through their shows and the discussions and strategies that were worked out within them. This is why, when looking back at the fundamental artistic movements of the last century, we immediately think of those gallery owners who promoted and supported them: Surrealism—Peggy Guggenheim and Julien Levy; Pop art—Leo Castelli; Fluxus—René Block; Arte Povera—Gian Enzo Sperone. These are just a few that immediately come to mind.

THE GALLERY AS A LIVING ORGANISM

Art galleries acquired new practices and functions during the twentieth century, closely related to the artistic languages on display within them. From mere storerooms for paintings and sculptures, as Durand-Ruel's and Kahnweiler's premises could have been described, galleries became places for installations, happenings, theater actions, and all manner of experimentation. Between the 1950s and the '70s, galleries were filled with all sorts of materials: coal and concrete, glass and gold, iron and steel, water and fire, ice and wind, earth and manure, and even absolutely nothing—not to mention a large number of living and dead animals, including horses, coyotes, parrots, donkeys, snakes, hens . . .

Whereas in the early years of the century, artists entered galleries to hang their paintings and place their sculptures, after World War II, they transformed these spaces into stages for an array of activities: They masturbated and slashed themselves, cooked, slept, and acted, they had themselves shot, slapped and bit each other, drew on the walls suspended from elastic cords, vomited, urinated, and acted like dogs on a leash. They stuck their gallery owner on the wall, as you can see on the cover of this book. An ironic, emblematic gesture this was—an act of rebellion by the artist against the overweening power of the gallerist, but actually it also shows the level of complicity that binds together these two key figures in the art system of our age.

In recent decades, the physical space of the gallery has become a material for artists to work with: Galleries have been perforated, sanded, flooded, burnt, stripped of their paint, deprived of their floors, sealed off, duplicated, destroyed, and declared closed. In other words, from a "vault" for artwork, the art gallery has become the content of the work, a place for discussion and experimentation, and an instrument for an infinite variety of statements.

THE GALLERIST TODAY

This is not the place to mention the names of the extraordinary number of gallery owners who have supported contemporary art with such passion, often helping to write the history of the art of our time—this list would be too long.

For this book, aside from a few exceptions, I have interviewed the generations of gallery owners who opened since the 1980s. While this is obviously only a partial selection, I have tried to include a series of personalities from around the world.

Some of them are very young, but they are already playing an important role.

From the interviews that follow, one thing appears to be quite clear: The ideal role of a gallerist remains something like what Kahnweiler pioneered at the beginning of the last century. He or she becomes the "traveling companion" of artists, ready to share creative and intellectual adventures, with passionate and intelligent devotion to their work. The economic success of a gallery is always a fundamental objective—it ensures its survival and proves its validity. Even so, money is not the main motivation for the most interesting gallery owners today; after all, other professions are more financially rewarding and less quixotic. As Turin-based gallery owner Franco Noero says here, "It's incredibly sexy trying to base an economy on poetry."

THE YOUNGEST GENERATIONS

The natural consequence of the recent expansion of the art world and its economy has been a remarkable increase in the number of art galleries, begun by people from a whole range of different backgrounds. But in the past ten years we have witnessed a new phenomenon: Increasingly, critics, art historians, independent curators, and artists are opening private art galleries. While the ranks of those working in contemporary art have swelled beyond the hiring capacity of museums and other institutions, private galleries also allow them a level of creative freedom and decision making that no public organization could ever offer. As Johann König, the young Berlin-based gallery owner, explains, his gallery gives him "the power to make things happen."

The youngest galleries—those that have opened in the past ten years—increasingly start out as project spaces, as seen in examples such as The Modern Institute in Glasgow, Vitamin Creative Space in China, Kurimanzutto in Mexico City, Castillo Corrales and gb agency in Paris, Raster and Foksal Foundation in Poland, T293 in Naples, the Breeder in Athens, Gregor Podnar in Slovenia, and Orchard Gallery (which closed in 2008) and Reena Spaulings Fine Art in New York.

In their interview, Carolina Dankow and Marina Leuenberger, the two founders of Karma International in Zurich, maintain that a rigid separation between an experimental space and a commercial gallery doesn't make much sense in the twenty-first century. In other words, the general trend appears to be toward not just a hybridization of roles (critics becoming gallery owners, artists working as critics, art-fair directors becoming museum curators, etc.) but also a hybridization of the gallery itself, as Solène Guillier and Nathalie Boutin of gb agency suggest.

The interviews in this book provide an extraordinary snapshot of today's art world, reflecting its culture, mood, and attitudes. Gallery owners talk about the world in which they work, their relationships with artists, and what they hate or, on the contrary, love most about their what they do. In many cases, they also give precious advice to young collectors about how to approach the creation of their own collections, as well as offering suggestions for potential young gallery owners and directors about how to build up their own programs, and how to find their way in this complex world. These are fascinating people, with smart ideas, and in the following pages they tell us about their early days and tackle topical issues, such as the role of contemporary art museums today.

Like *Collecting Contemporary Art*, the series of interviews with collectors that I coedited for JRP|Ringier, the idea behind this book has been to make a contribution, however partial, to a greater understanding of the contemporary art world, and it is an invitation to share together this creative and intellectual adventure.

Andrea Bellini

H

K

M

N

P

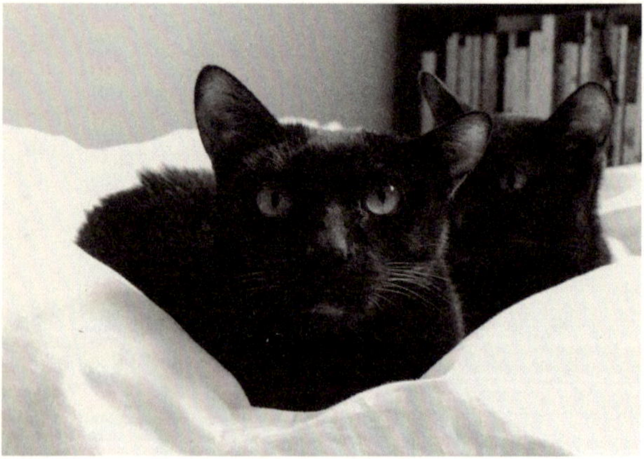

Air de Paris

Florence Bonnefous

AIR DE PARIS, PARIS

— You met Edouard Merino in the second half of the 1980s, at the École du Magasin in Grenoble, Europe's first school for curators. I imagine you were both thinking of becoming independent curators. How did you decide to open a gallery in Nice?

Just after we met, we decided to do a project together, and we were absolutely of one mind. We didn't have much chance of working together other than by opening a gallery, although we didn't have a very clear idea of what we were embarking upon.

— I think you've helped open up and transform the very concept of the art gallery, turning a commercial arena into a sort of miniature Kunsthalle. Were you aware of this at the time?

As I was saying, we didn't really know what we were doing—we just did it. We were living "in real time." The idea was to maintain a certain freedom—quality of life—and to move ahead quickly, although without impossible ambitions. We were driven by a fair share of pride and the desire to be different.

— It could be said that your first exhibitions have entered the annals of art history. "*Les Ateliers du Paradis*" in 1990 comes to mind, the first exhibition to take up the idea of relational art, with Philippe Parreno, Pierre Joseph, and Philippe Perrin. How did the idea for that exhibition come about?

I don't really remember—possibly in a café in Grenoble, or was it in Venice during a walk along the shore on the day before "*Courts métrages immobiles*" (Motionless Short Films) opened at the Biennale that year? With the technical specifications that the artists had given us, the exhibition was a sort of extension, inside a gallery, of what we were experiencing on the outside. And it certainly laid the foundations for our activity, and our way of taking it forward—its spirit, in other words.

— How was it that the group that formed around you developed and then theorised relational aesthetics? I'm thinking, for example, of your friendship with Eric Troncy and Nicolas Bourriaud.

We aren't theoreticians; we're friends of theoreticians. I was already friends with Troncy, and Edouard with Bourriaud, and we all just came together. The group formed very quickly. Liam Gillick came to the gallery one day—this was in 1990, when the gallery was still in Nice. He was Angela Bulloch's boyfriend. And it was there that he met Parreno, Joseph, and Troncy; then came Carsten Höller and Nikolaus Schafhausen in '91. And so on . . . like circles in water, within the space of two years.

— What do you think of relational art today?

Relational aesthetics was a very useful instrument in those days, for it showed the work of an ensemble of artists (more than of a clearly defined group, as might be the case today); like all sharp instruments, it gets blunt.

— As you say, the gallery immediately started with an excellent group of artists, the ensemble you mentioned. Did you also make some mistakes? Were there any decisions you wouldn't make today?

The greatest mistake was certainly that of opening a gallery. I don't know if I would do it again . . . but what else could I do? Keep in mind a fantastic bunch of artists we spent some magical moments with: Bruno Serralongue, who is also my partner; Trisha Donnelly, who became a very dear friend; Paul McCarthy, with whom we had some unforgettable adventures; Jean-Luc Verna and Brice Dellsperger; Rob Pruitt, whom we met in '91, lost sight of, and then ended up working with again.

— I have heard that no artist has ever left your gallery. What sort of relationship do you have with artists?

It's probably our absolute sincerity that makes us appealing. We're idiots who have never exploited artists, or if we have, it has been quite unintentional. We have never fawned over them or adulated them.

This means they have confidence in us, even though we're not the gallery that gets the most possible money for them. We are interested in their projects more than in the money these projects might bring.

— Visiting your gallery is always a revelation. You've rediscovered long-forgotten artists, such as Guy de Cointet, with almost philological passion.
The thrill of the investigation and the power of evocation! It is also, in part, a reaction to the prevailing desire to appear young. We would always like to be seen as a young gallery that also shows older artists. We try to make sure that the search for pleasure is included in all the nooks and crannies of our intellect, especially when it appears to be an increasingly improbable and impossible task.

Olivier Antoine

ART : CONCEPT, PARIS

— Tell me about the early years. What was your educational background? What brought you to art?
I grew up in the south of France, in Saint Paul de Vence. I think the ambience of the village in the 1970s–'80s—with the Maeght Foundation, and all the great art at La Colombe d'Or restaurant as well as the education I received from my parents, certainly fired up my interest in artistic creation. I did a lot of different things before opening a gallery, including trying to be an artist. To cut a long story short, I finished my law studies and then went to Nice to meet the best artists and to get to know the local art scene.

— You opened your first gallery there, in Nice, in 1992. You once told me that your initial program was to a certain degree a disaster—you didn't yet have a clear idea of what an art gallery should or could be. How did you become a successful gallery owner? What were the meetings and opportunities that turned your gallery into one of the most interesting in France?

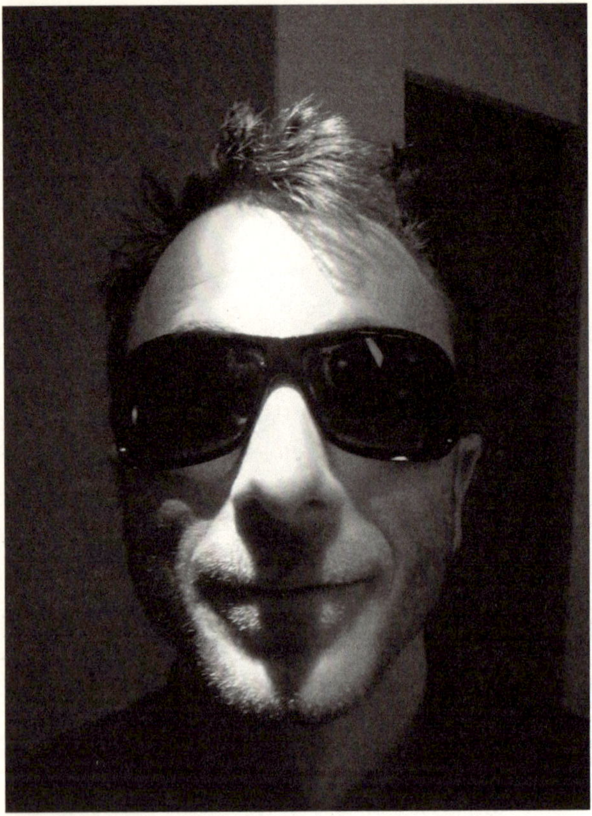

Olivier Antoine
Photo: Vidya & Jérome

After starting to produce publications, engravings, lithographs, and other types of prints, I opened a little space to show them. It was extremely tough, and it didn't last long. From prints, I moved to original works on paper, and I moved to a larger space. In 1992, I invited Jean-Yves Jouannais to put on the opening exhibition of the new gallery. It was called "Fiasco." I personally had the impression that "Fiasco" was a form of resistance against success and efficiency. Even though a long time has gone by since that exhibition, I'm still rather doubtful when I see some people's success and what that success leads to. Maintaining that sort of position involves actions that I don't ever want to be involved with. We printed a little plate by Erik Dietman for the occasion, which stated: "Failure is the only way not to err." I love that phrase. After that, I alternated showing solo and group exhibitions depending on how much money I had at the time. Then in '97, I joined the 13th arrondissement project in Paris.[1]

— You work with a group of interesting young artists, but they're all very different from each other. How do you choose your artists?

That's something I always wonder about. My aim is to draw up a program that relates to the world and its complexity. It doesn't bother me if a work is or isn't in line with an aesthetic current; I'm interested in its content. I avoid all useless words, I just try to understand the politics of the work—what the artist is aiming to express in that particular form. Sometimes it takes years to understand, so I just have to trust my instinct when making a decision. Even so, most artists I work with have a very simple relationship with things; their artwork always remains on a human level. I try to represent artists whose works adopt a language that is common to all cultures. As I see it, there isn't one particular aesthetic form that's better than another. The meaning of a work is primeval, and the shape of a work is no more than its crystallization, or the fossilization of thought. The gallery exhibitions are a sort of comment on the contemporary world, and yet each exhibition is like one episode in a long story that is constantly being written.

— What sort of relationship do you have with your artists? Do you interact at the project level, or do you just encourage them in their work in general?
That's a delicate question you're asking. I hope I have a close relationship with the gallery's artists, as close as possible but without interfering with their work. In any case, I'm at their disposal if they need advice or motivation, and I help them. My experience leads me to believe that all artists have ambitions, but they need to be moderated—they

mustn't sacrifice their works on the altar of success. An artist may spend twenty years producing a work, and why not? It is fantastic to work on such long-term projects.

— Even though you're young, you have considerable experience as a gallery owner. Describe the ideal collector.
Well, I would say the ideal collector, as I see it, is one who builds up a collection that resists simply being trendy. Another fundamental aspect of a collection is that it should be seen, even though it doesn't necessarily have to be public.

— In 1997, you moved to the capital. For years, Paris was on the fringes of the contemporary art world, but recently it seems to be picking up, once again acquiring a central role. How do you view the city today?
To answer this question I would like to paraphrase the group Présence Panchounette: "Things have evolved since Darwin." I mean, I'm very happy to see the interest and attention this city is attracting, but we have to be realistic. Paris is a small city in Europe compared to the new cities in developing countries. It can't play a central role because there aren't any real centers any more: Globalization has made every place a suburb. It's also a city where

public expenditure includes "reception costs"—as if civil society depended on buffets, aperitifs, and banquets of an opulence on a par with the decorations at the Opéra Garnier. And Paris has always been like that—just read Balzac or Zola; habits really haven't changed. What is fantastic, though, and what will be the future of this city, is the emergence of a new generation of creative talents who are far more open to the international scene than their older siblings ever were. For some years now, many foreigners have come to live in Paris, and this new lifeblood gives dynamism to the city. Will this new intelligentsia resist the appeal of buffet dinners, preferring to get a bike and ride around the city? But actually, it doesn't really matter because, in spite of everything, and all the criticisms notwithstanding, Paris is still one of the most pleasant cities in the world.

— What was your best intuition? And your worst mistake?
That God doesn't exist, and repeating that too often.

— Would you agree with Tobias Meyer of Sotheby's, who told *Der Spiegel* that the most expensive works of art are the best ones?
From what point of view? I don't want to dwell on that sort of statement. In a few years' time we'll

see how sales have gone in the first decade of the twenty-first century—the great rock-'n'-roll swindle!

— Are you worried about the current financial crisis? Did you sell less in 2008 than in the previous year?
Surprisingly, 2008 was a good year, but I can't say anything about the future of the gallery, as 2009 is certainly going to be tough. I just want to keep my precious collaborators close to me, and do everything possible to continue the gallery's program. But I'm very worried about the current situation from a human point of view. The financial crisis is simply the visible part of a global problem. We must create a society where life based on work and ecology rather than simply financial values. And this will require a change in lifestyle. We're on the threshold of an age of radical change, an evolution of the human species. The question remains the same: What future are we giving our kids? Or rather: What culture are we handing down to them? Fear and consumption?

[1] In 1997 six galleries (Art : Concept, Air de Paris, Jennifer Flay, Emmanuel Perrotin, Praz-Delavallade and Almine Rech) decided to join their mailing-lists and to organize simultaneous openings.

Daniele Balice

BALICEHERTLING, PARIS

— Daniele, you are yet another example of a young Italian who escapes from his own country and seeks his fortune abroad—like curators Massimiliano Gioni, Francesco Manacorda, and Luca Cerizza, gallery owners Isabella Bortolozzi and Jennifer Chert, as well as a number of artists. What led you to leave Bari?

I've often wondered about this, but the answer is simple: I have a tendency to be a nomad; the idea of being sedentary frightened me even when I was a child. I came here by a pretty roundabout way. After high school, I went to Paris to study art, then went back briefly to Milan, where I cut my teeth at *Flash Art*. After this crucial experience, I went to New York for four and a half years and then came back to Paris. I've always been worried about spending my life in just one city, and I left Bari as soon as I could, without any particular resentment but with a burning curiosity to see the rest of the world.

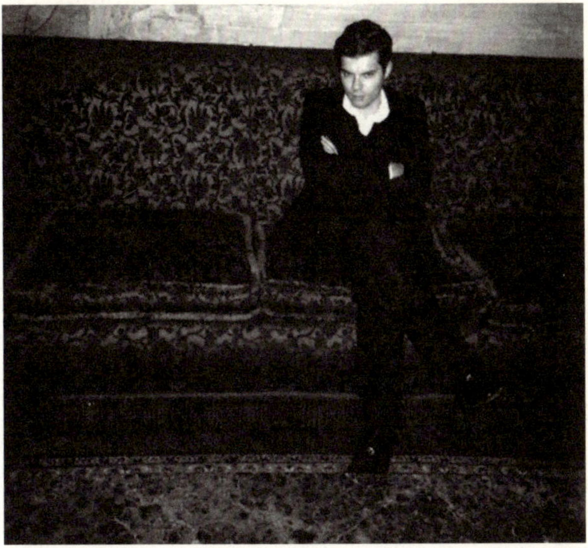

Daniele Balice

— I met you in New York in 2004—I was starting to work as the US editor of *Flash Art*, while you were with a private gallery in Williamsburg. I may be wrong, but at the time you didn't seem all that sure about what you wanted to do in life. The gallery you were working for wasn't exactly mainstream, and I sort of had the feeling you didn't want to expose yourself too much—you almost seemed to be hiding. And yet I imagine that's where your first important contacts with collectors started. Is that right?

You're right. My time in Williamsburg came immediately after another, completely different experience in a gallery on the Upper East Side, in the office of a ruthless modern-art dealer, who seemed to be a character straight out of *Gossip Girl*. Williamsburg was a more "underground" experience, at a time when people believed anything was possible in the art market. These two experiences were totally discreet, not so much as a strategy of mine, but because I was shy, and I wanted to observe, find out, and learn as much as possible.
New York was mainly a time of study for me, and I experienced it as a spectator, not as a protagonist. My encounters with collectors and artists had naturally started already, but in an absolutely natural way, with no ulterior motives. I think I managed to build up some good friendships with some of them, and they are still very important today in the decisions for the gallery program: Bill Cournoyer, for example, is a young New York collector who has accompanied my career with great generosity and lots of useful advice.

— How did you decide to leave New York and move to Paris? That's the opposite of the usual migration.
I wanted to get back to Europe, and Paris is certainly the city that best complements New York, even though it's totally different. The quality of life is fantastic,

and I can concentrate on research, reading, and thinking. It was a fundamental step to make after the frantic years in New York. The city offers a huge amount in terms of culture, and the possibilities are endless. Paris is unjustly underestimated by the contemporary art world, but it's in continuous movement. And I must say that going a bit against the current is never all that much of a bad thing.

— Working with Olivier Antoine at Art : Concept must have been a formative experience.
Working at Art : Concept allowed me to try out my network and to give visibility to some artists whose work I appreciated. I brought Gedi Sibony, Ulla von Brandenburg, Annelise Coste, and Adam McEwen to Olivier's fold, along with many others, and they gave a more cosmopolitan focus to the gallery. The first difference I noticed between working in New York and working in Paris was the way your work is appreciated: In New York, you're justly rewarded and paid for a job well done, whereas in Paris, you need to cope with the egocentrism and jealousies of the various micro-communities in the art world. Parisian galleries like Air de Paris and Chantal Crousel have obtained international success by building up a more open community, which is closely linked to the gallery's commercial activities, and they are now our model. I don't think that's coincidental.

— Last year, you decided to make a bold leap and open a gallery of your own. It really did start out on the quiet, with you even deciding to share tiny premises (on alternate months) with a curious collective, Castillo Corrales. I must say that initially it seemed like a rather unusual choice: I thought you were running the risk of ending up in anonymity, not being sufficiently visible because of this on-and-off presence in the area. But it proved to be the right choice. The crisis came, and your slightly underground, low-profile model aroused a great deal of interest. Why did you choose the Belleville quarter, and was your decision to share the premises simply economic?

In the early years of the gallery, we wanted to invest in the works of artists, and not just in the packaging. In the years of the economic boom in the art market, there were too many gallery directors and curators who took over the work of artists. Discovering an artist became an act of expropriation—not just economically, but intellectually too. This attitude still exists, but it has been mitigated by the crisis. So, to start off, we decided to share the space with Castillo Corrales, a collective that includes Oscar Tuazon, one of our artists. The aim wasn't just to cut costs but to invest as much as possible in the creation of stunning exhibitions. Even though the premises are tiny, they are perfect for young artists,

because they can concentrate on a more precise project. I would say we favored essentiality over quantity, and we reduced the presence of the gallery owner in order to focus on the artists—without whom we wouldn't exist.
The choice of Belleville was the result of both sentimental and practical reasons: Galleries like Jocelyn Wolff and Cosmic have been working in the district for a number of years, and, of course, Le Plateau provides an institutional presence. But I can unashamedly admit that the area also offers superb restaurants, a very lively local life, two beautiful parks, and is relatively close to the city centre. The Centre Pompidou is just a few stops away on the metro, and the rue de Belleville is full of taxis until late in evening. This quarter is lively seven days a week, thanks to the various communities that make it quite different from any other in the city. In a certain sense, it reminds me of New York's Lower East Side and, to an extent, Naples too, with all its chaotic energy.

— In just a short time, you and your working partner Alexander Hertling had one of the coolest galleries in town. I think that's thanks to your program. How do you choose your artists?
I would like to say the success of the gallery is mainly due to the artists who have accepted and understood

our project. As I was saying, from the way things started out, it didn't seem as though we were going to achieve instant economic success, yet it worked out really well. Falke Pisano was just in the Venice Biennale, and Art Basel accepting us into the Statements and Unlimited sections. The press have given us amazing support, reviewing every single exhibition we've put on.

The choice of artists is based on constant interaction between me, Alexander, and our network of friends and artists. I also think our experiences abroad have enabled us to come up with a more transversal and open taste. I should also mention that the gallery has the collaboration of Pati Hertling, Alexander's twin sister, who lives in New York. She's a lawyer by day but a curator by night, organizing nonprofit events at Gavin Brown's Enterprise, and she brings together a number of people from the art world in New York. Many of our artists, such as Kerstin Braetsch, Reto Pulfer, and Nikolas Gambaroff, are part of the community around Pati. We started out on the quiet, and our relative shyness let the public concentrate on the work of the artists, who are the only people who deserve any credit.

— Alexander comes from the world of fashion, but he's now working full time at the gallery. How do you collaborate?

He was born and grew up in Berlin, so Alexander has long been absorbing visual input from great artists. His opinion is part of every decision, and the fact that he is new to the market often means he has a purer approach to the work of young artists. In a certain sense, he is more open than I am. I must admit that he has a far more sophisticated sense of space than I do, and the way he arranges the works in an exhibition is fantastic.
His background in the world of fashion is also quite exceptional, and he worked for designers who were often closer to the world of art than to that of fashion. For a number of years, he worked on producing events and fashion parades for designers such as Raf Simons, Veronique Branquinho, Bernard Wilhelm, and Walter Van Beirendock.

— What was your best intuition? And your biggest regret?
My best intuition was when I was young, and I sensed the resignation in people all around me. I reacted by accepting the risky consequences of doing what I wanted to do in life, and as a result, I have absolutely no regrets.

— Your policy was successful right from the start. Can you give five pieces of advice to a young person who wants to open a gallery today?

I probably ought to wait and answer this question in a few years' time, but I'll try:

1. Take the risk of starting with artists no one else wants to work with.
2. Don't draw up a business plan.
3. Work with young collectors and help them grow with the gallery.
4. Avoid aesthetic uniformity in your program.
5. Never make any sort of compromise.

— Seeing as you're so good in this, what would you suggest to a young person who's thinking of collecting contemporary art?

If I were a young collector, I would concentrate on collaborating with young galleries, and I would develop a relationship based on trust and interaction. This doesn't mean buying solely in young galleries but creating an intellectual rapport that can help build up the collection in a healthy and intelligent way. Going to art fairs is crucial, especially ones like Art Basel, Frieze, and Artissima, which don't have speculators concealed within them. Reading is fine, but not just from specialized magazines: To understand the work of the contemporary artist, you need to be interested in everything and open to all sources. This may be what helps a collector stay forever young—contemporary art is a sort of mental gymnastics.

Isabella Bortolozzi

GALERIE ISABELLA BORTOLOZZI, BERLIN

— You opened your gallery in Berlin in 2004, just five years ago, and it has already become one of the city's benchmark galleries. Everyone knows that Germany is no easy place for an outsider, so how did you manage to fit in so well and so rapidly in such a tough and competitive environment?
I already had a good command of German.

— On the door of your first gallery there was a large, hand-painted question mark. What was it? A statement about art, or about life in general?
Július Koller stuck the question mark on the door. We both wanted visitors to open a door with a question mark on it and then find at least another fifty more when they entered. I thought it was a good starting point.

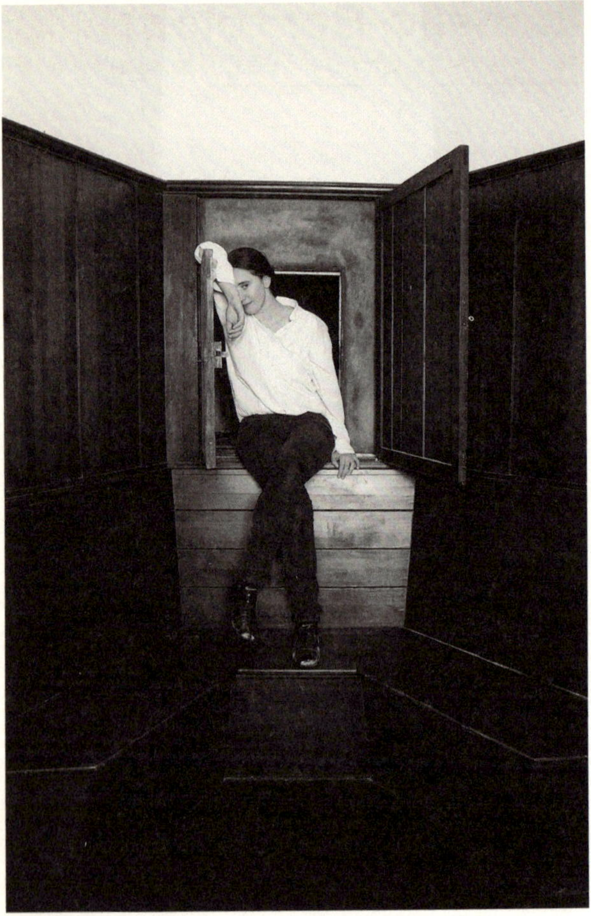

Isabella Bortolozzi

— You worked as a gallery assistant for Sonia Rosso in Turin. What is your educational background?
I started with Sonia and with Franco Noero. I'm a translator.

— From a professional point of view, what have been your most important encounters?
The ones I've had with my artists.

— German art—and painting, in particular—has enjoyed huge commercial success in recent years. You opened a gallery in Berlin and for a few years you didn't represent a single German artist.
I now represent two German artists, Nora Schultz and Michael S. Riedel, and neither of them paints.

— You opened your gallery with an exhibition of work by Július Koller, the legendary Slovak artist. Why him?
Because Julius was an "Ufonaut."

— What mistake do you wish you'd never made?
I'm too young, I haven't made any yet that are that memorable! I'm bound to make some—we'll see.

— A question about the city. Many people maintain that Berlin has become contemporary art capital simply because of its cheap rents. Would you agree? What other factors are involved?

I wouldn't agree. Rent is one factor, but it's not fundamental. A constantly expanding community of artists, young curators, and critics, and serious magazines—it's this, and much more besides, that makes Berlin one of the European capitals of contemporary art.

— One last thing: Tell me what sort of collector you really can't stand. So anyone reading this book will know whether or not to come see you in Berlin.
Those who show their muscles.

Gavin Brown

GAVIN BROWN'S ENTERPRISE, NEW YORK

— Last year, you were on a panel organized by the Art Dealers Association of America, whose title posed the question, "Is the Killer Art Market Killing Art?" A silly question, but in the course of the discussion, you made a couple interesting points. By discovering young artists and exhibiting them, you argued, gallery owners are now doing the work of curators. You also posited that art fairs have become a new model for exhibitions. In other words, if something is going to be killed, it isn't art but curators and contemporary art museums.

I don't know if anyone is going to get killed. Art is never killed or captured. It is constantly moving and escaping from capital. It is ethereal and everywhere.

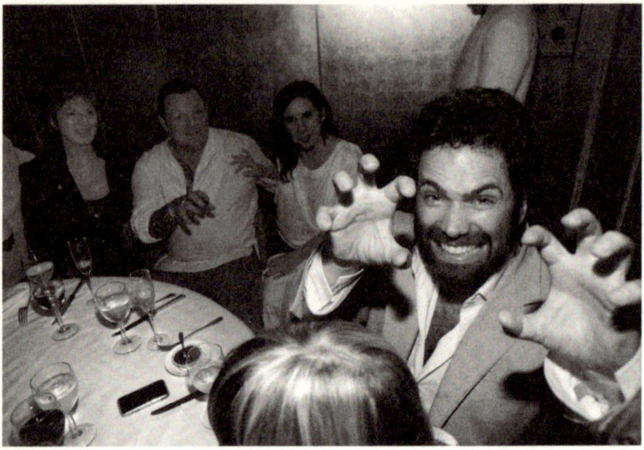

From left: Eva Presenhuber, Urs Fischer, Cassandra McCloud, Gavin Brown

In terms of art fairs and curators and galleries and museums: Those are all business categories; they don't have relevance to art. If they are no longer engaged in the arena where art resides at this moment, then they may keep living, but they will no longer be with art. This process can be very slow and hard to see until it has passed.

— Who is Gavin Brown? What did you study, and how did you get into the art world?
I don't know who I am. That is an ongoing process. I think about it all the time. The biographical facts to date: He was born in the UK. Went to school in the UK.

Moved to the US aged twenty-three to study. Stayed. Had children there. Lives there now. As for the art world: Studied art. Worked in galleries. Made art. Met artists. Sold art. Still selling art.

— Your luckiest encounter? Is there someone who helped change your view of the world?
Many, many people. Many things. Artists and artworks. Buildings and books.

— Your greatest intuition, and also your greatest mistake?
I don't believe in mistakes—only experience that you learn from or not.

— I have heard that you let Maurizio Cattelan escape you. Is that true?
Just like art, Maurizio cannot be captured and so cannot escape.

— How long can you stay on the crest of the wave as a gallery owner? Is it a job with a fixed cycle?
The "job" comes in many forms, many species—like flowers or insects. Their life cycles vary just as much. Some galleries can be successful and thrive—within their terms—for many, many years. Others are, by definition, here for shorter periods. They bloom brightly and strongly and then die suddenly.

The difficult process is to transform from one species to another—from a bug with the life cycle of a day to a sequoia that lives for millennia and is an ecosystem in itself.

— What do you hate most about the art system? And what could you never do without?

I hate travel. Tours. Watching us all get older in the same old places.

I could never do without my friends.

— What would you have done if you hadn't become a gallery owner?

No one else would have employed me, so I had to give myself a job. I dread to think of my life had I gone another way.

— And what will you do after?

Read, and hopefully live long enough to see my grandchildren and, god willing, great-grandchildren.

Mario Cristiani Lorenzo Fiaschi Maurizio Rigillo

GALLERIACONTINUA,
SAN GIMIGNANO, BEIJING, LE MOULIN

— You have an incredible story. Let me sum it up briefly: You've been friends since high school, and in 1990 you decided to open a gallery in a garage in San Gimignano, a little town in the province of Siena. Apart from Lorenzo, who was studying at the Accademia di Belli Arti in Florence at the time, none of you had any experience at all in the art world. You started out with a capital of one million lire each—which equals a total of 2,500 euros today. After just a few years, you had attracted enormous attention, in Italy and abroad. Now you also have a gallery in Beijing and an exhibition space just outside Paris, and you take part in the most important art fairs around the world with an extraordinary group of artists. Could you tell me the secret of your success?

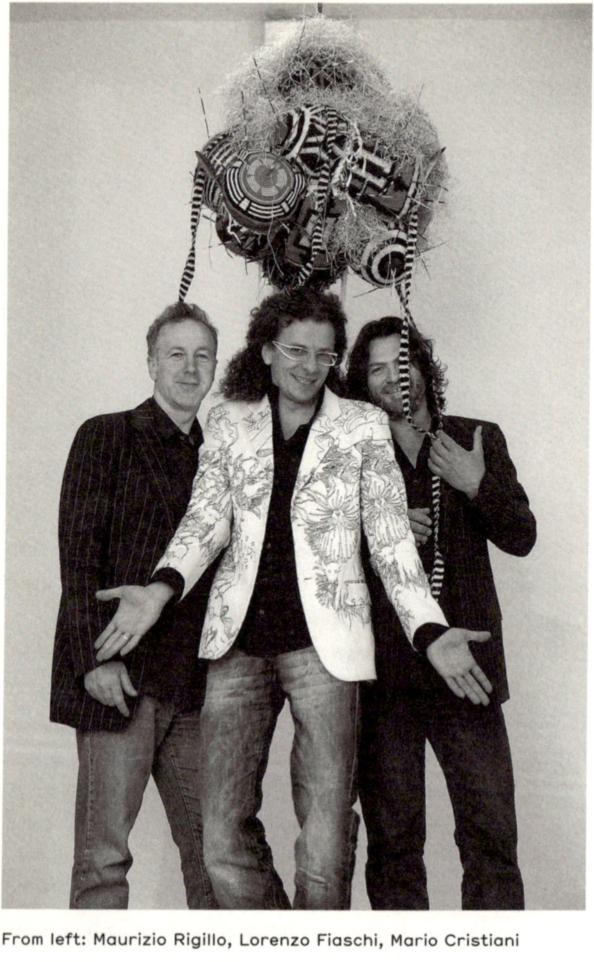

From left: Maurizio Rigillo, Lorenzo Fiaschi, Mario Cristiani

All sorts of factors contributed to this. One thing is certain, and it is that nothing was worked out beforehand. When we started we had no clear objectives—we just had a huge amount of energy, passion, and a pinch of healthy craziness, which meant we could bring about real changes. We've always maintained our initial spirit, because we're still convinced that there is no ultimate goal, just an endless road. We've had our share of difficulties like everyone else, of course, but we've tried to turn them into our strong points by working hard and with great conviction.

— Right at the beginning you created two different units: GALLERIACONTINUA and the Arte Continua association. Why was that?

We wanted to try being together while respecting our different backgrounds, and we were bound by our friendship and the pleasure of sharing great moments and adventures, thanks to our shared passion for contemporary art. We've always tried to remain loyal to the work of the artist, both when we are working on a project in the gallery and when working on projects created and promoted by the association we founded, and we work on these together with public institutions in Italy and abroad. Right from the outset, we were convinced that we should aim for international standards in art. And we wanted to keep the two levels

on which we had decided to work quite separate: that of our own freedom of choice and approach—and of the gallery's survival, in economic terms—and that of interacting with institutions and promoting art throughout the world. This is why we started Arte all'Arte, the Rinascimento Nascimento project, and the artexvino=acqua campaign. We wanted absolute clarity and the shouldering of responsibilities, for we were convinced that this could be a real point of encounter between the need for individual freedom and the need to bring the most important expressions of contemporary art into places that belonged to everyone. We chose a place where both artists and other leading figures in the world of art could find an area for cooperation rather than competition, compensating for a lack of initiative by the public administration, which was much felt in those days. We always involved curators in these initiatives, together with other artists who were never those who actually worked in the gallery. If some artists decided to stay, they only did so afterward.
The aim was to adopt a certain approach, which many years later became fashionable under the name of "corporate social responsibility." We love art, and we are the first to take on the duty and honor of supporting it in every way possible, while always respecting the law. It didn't seem, and it still doesn't seem right to us that public spaces should

be outsourced or run as though they were a burden to be offloaded onto the first person who's willing to take it on free of charge (or, even better, if it's a friend of this or that administrator), without any real selection criteria. What is done in this field has effects not just on today's generations, but also on those who will come in the future. If there hadn't been people in the past who, like us, believed in and were committed to their contemporaries—people like Benozzo Gozzoli, Taddeo di Bartolo, Simone Martini, and so many others—today neither we nor the tourists who flock to San Gimignano would have the pleasure of being surrounded by these masterpieces, and being able to see them without fees to pay, as so often occurs today. We've tried to make sure we can act on a number of different levels. We do this by acting firmly and resolutely both on the private and on the nonprofit and public level. We're simply responding to the contemporary with the contemporary.

— Tell me about how it all started. What processes, what joint ventures, and what contacts allowed you to grow so rapidly?

Actually, our growth wasn't that rapid—we had plenty of hills to climb! The public found it hard to believe in three young people who wanted to bring contemporary art into what was considered the cradle of classical art. Since we're allergic to pre-packaged ideas and situations, we trusted our instinct. The first people who put their confidence in us were Elio Grazioli and Luciano Pistoi. They became real friends, good advisers, and great companions on our adventures. After them, there were lots of people who liked us and accompanied us on our early ventures. And the rest came down to the work: ours and that of the artists.

— Arte all'Arte is possibly one of the most interesting environmental art projects to have appeared in recent years in Italy, and possibly in Europe. You thought it up and produced it with your own money. How did the project start, and why did it come to an end?
Arte all'Arte was started with Luciano Pistoi during one of our countless meetings at his home, where we would talk for hours and hours about art, artists, and potential or visionary projects. For years, Luciano had been organizing an annual meeting at Castello di Volpaia, and we decided to go further, putting together a project that would be a minor revolution, leaving a tangible sign of its passing on the land. What we were hoping to do was to create new development models that would bring together culture, production, and environmental protection. For more than ten years, between 1995 and 2005, we tried to create a new balance between the city and the countryside through the works of artists, in some cases

leaving works permanently. At a certain point, we felt that our task had come to an end, and that the ball we had set rolling could continue on its own. It still remains a model that can be started up again, and we hope that this will occur in other situations, and other lands.

— A few years ago, you launched the artexvino=acqua charitable project, as a way of funding humanitarian projects in various parts of the world.

Our aim was to show how art can be used to unite and reassess relationships, even simply through an exchange of resources and values that enriches both sides. Mario Merz, when he was here with his wife Marisa in 2002, said on his way to the cathedral to see the frescoes, "I'm going off to see a bit of dust on the walls." This could only have been said by an artist who was capable of transforming dust into stunning visions, which others then took and loved. Artexvino=acqua is no more than a variation on this idea. With wine, and with the contribution of these transforming magicians—the artists—we were able to take water to those who had none. The project is a simple formula in which art is used as an element of connection and reflection, and, it becomes an instrument through which we can pass from a local to a global dimension, taking water to dramatically parched areas of our planet.

The project brings together six great international artists, invited by Vincente Todoli, and six of Italy's most exquisite wines, selected by chef Antonello Colonna. This was a highly significant encounter that gave rise to an extremely small series of wines, with exclusive labels made by the artists involved. Specially made for the occasion, these labels were in fact signed and numbered prints and lithographs. The funds collected during the charity campaign were used entirely for water-supply projects, which have so far brought relief in Brazil, India, Senegal, Palestine, China, and Ghana. The money raised through events in 2009 will be donated to the Grameen Bank to assist its micro-credit system, the brainchild of the Nobel Peace Prize winner Muhammad Yunus, who in recent years has provided thousands of families with loans for their small businesses. Our aim is to strengthen a virtuous circle that is destined never to run out, and to raise even greater awareness, renewing our commitment to achieve territorial balance.

— You are philanthropists and you work with sincere passion, so you are the ideal people to ask for advice for a young collector approaching the world of art at a time of international crisis.

Love life and love art. Go regularly to exhibitions, art fairs, museums, biennials, and places of art, because understanding and education are fundamental to becoming a good collector. And read up on everything—in books, magazines, reviews, and catalogues—in order to understand how art and the market are moving, so that you can choose your own direction quite independently.

Invest your time by talking with artists, gallery directors, and other collectors, because it is through this sort of interaction that you will learn.

Trust in your own intuition and purchase only what you really like.

Don't invest in the works of artists who are too well established—take pleasure in a gamble, even with yourself, by purchasing those of emerging artists, with the hope that you will be able to develop together!

Chantal Crousel

GALERIE CHANTAL CROUSEL, PARIS

— How did you start? What was the spark that ignited your passion for art?

When I was twenty-three, I didn't know anything about contemporary art. I entered a "shop" that had a single, beautiful little drawing in the window, and I left the gallery with that small Man Ray drawing under my arm—that was the spark. I decided to make of this encounter my profession: to understand, explain, and convey the knowledge and the value of works of art. Consequently, I studied art history and got some experience in three years as a gallery assistant. And between 1976 and 1979, together with a fellow graduate from my course, Jacques Blazy, we created La Dérive, a gallery that combined exquisite primitive artworks and contemporary art.

— You started in 1980 with Tony Cragg, and now you're working with a series of important young artists, such as Jennifer Allora & Guillermo Calzadilla, Darren Almond, Claire Fontaine, Wade Guyton, Melik Ohanian, Anri Sala, and Reena Spaulings, to name but a few.

In other words, with thirty years of history behind you, you are still able to capture the zeitgeist. How do you choose your artists?
In 1980, Tony Cragg was a very young artist who wanted to reflect the essence of his time and the ongoing changes in society, and to do this in a language that was totally new and original, breaking with the previous generation of sculptors—Henry Moore and others. With his own formal vocabulary, he introduced a new form of beauty, of aesthetics that had not existed before. These very qualities are what I have always been looking for with every artist I have added to the gallery prkogram.

— You work with a number of artists who often use video. Are you particularly interested in that medium?
Video is a very powerful form of expression. Video art has a different language from that of television and the cinema, but it shares their fascination with the moving image. The artists I am most interested in are often multimedia artists. They make video works when video is the most pertinent medium to express what they want to say. This is the case with artists like Anri Sala, Melik Ohanian, Allora & Calzadilla, Gabriel Orozco, and most of our artists. Although in November we will have the first gallery exhibition of Wang Bing, a Chinese artist who only works in video.

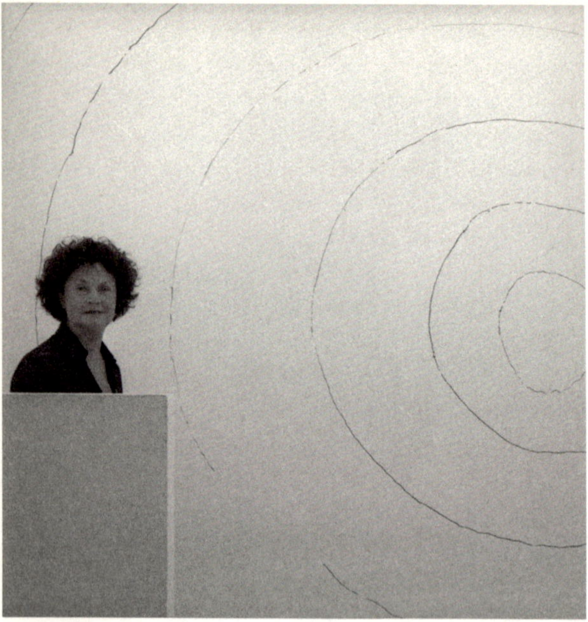

Chantal Crousel
Photo: Alberto Garcia-Alix

— You're considered a passionate, scrupulous, and highly successful gallery owner, but you've also had to deal with some pretty tough economic times. How did you manage to start up again after the crisis of the early '90s?

At the beginning of the 1990s, I was in a fifty-fifty partnership with the Robelin family. The gallery's name at that time was Crousel-Robelin/Bama. When in 1991–92 our turnover dropped dramatically, my associates wanted to close down the gallery; I did not. They pulled out their part of the capital, and their bank guarantee. I continued. Those were very hard times, but also exciting years, during which I did the first exhibitions of Gabriel Orozco, Mona Hatoum, Rirkrit Tiravanija, and others.

— With your long experience, how do you view today's economic crisis, and how are you dealing with it? Are there differences between the market collapse in the late '80s and the current one?

The current economic crisis is different from the one in the early '90s. The gallery is strong. Our artists are among the most important and promising of their respective generations, and none of them is or has been subject to blind speculation. The market has become far more spread out. We have the confidence of collectors, and our artists are aware of the importance of making only necessary, irreplaceable work.

— What was your best hunch, and what was your worst mistake?

It is too early to talk about that.

— Tell me what a collector should never do when dealing with you. What approach do you detest the most.

I detest it when a buyer becomes vulgar or cynical about the value of a work when negotiating a reasonable and fair price for an excellent work, especially when he very much wants that work.

— What advice would you give a young person who is just beginning to collect?

1. See as many exhibitions as possible, to educate your eye and acquire a notion of contemporary history.
2. Try to understand what intrigues you in a work, even if you are disturbed by it. Beauty is a personal, evolving experience. It changes with time and history.
3. Find out, from experienced and trustworthy professionals, about the artist's place in the contemporary art context as well as his value on the market.
4. Focus on buying from the primary market. The secondary market may come later, to complete gaps in an already well-structured collection.

Thomas Dane

THOMAS DANE GALLERY, LONDON

— You opened your gallery in March 2004, but you started working in the art world about ten years before that. What was your educational background before that? And how did you start working in the art world?

I studied at University College London, and started dealing privately just after graduating in 1990. I worked discreetly with collectors in the UK and abroad, but keeping in close contact with artist friends whose work I collected and helped place and finance. I helped organize and fund, with Tamara Chodzko-Dial, Damien Hirst's "In and Out of Love" butterfly show in 1991, and continued to be involved with various contemporary artists in London, most notably Michael Landy.

In 1995, I founded Ridinghouse with Kartsen Schubert and Charles Asprey. We had an exhibition space for a few years and continued to publish editions and books after that. In 2000, I was one of three "angels" helping The Project gallery to restart in Harlem, New York. Then in 2001, I started working with Steve McQueen, and the gallery became a natural progression from this.

— We all owe our success to some important encounters. What have yours been? Who was it that helped you become what you've become?
There are some key encounters with artists that have definitely changed my life—Peter Doig, Michael Landy, Steve McQueen, to name but a few. A hugely important friend and colleague has been Ivor Braka, a private dealer in London, as well as Dimitris Daskalopoulos and Dimitris Paleocrassas in Greece. And then, in more recent years, my partners in the gallery, Martine d'Anglejan-Chatillon and François Chantala. I should also add the great support from collectors Anita and Poju Zabludowicz.

— Your gallery has been open for just five years, and yet the list of artists you work with is already quite extraordinary. I remember you opened the gallery in Duke Street with a solo show by Steve McQueen. How do you choose the artists you work with?

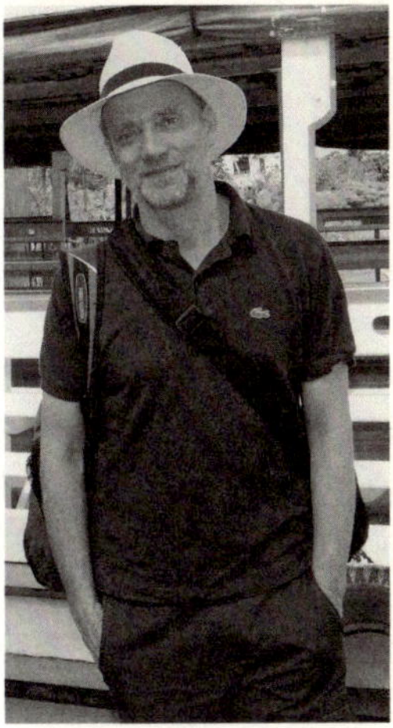

Thomas Dane

It is indeed a singular position. Because I was involved in the art world for a considerable time before opening the gallery, I had this group of friends and artists whom I trusted and who trusted me. They were primarily of my generation. They were initially the core of the program—Steve McQueen, Michael Landy, Paul Pfeiffer. Then the list of artists evolved through many different circumstances, mostly through my relationships with other dealers, curators, and artists of the gallery. In the last four years, choices are made very much as a team with Martine and François.

— You have a pretty complex and rather curious program, and sometimes you show historic works, as in the case of the Alexander Calder exhibition. What's the reasoning behind this?

I don't want the program to have too much of a strict conceptual or formal structure. I don't want to convey a message, or a rigid identity. The focus is more on the artists. We look across mediums, countries, and try to identify the artists whose work we admire and value most. And personal relationships are key. There has to be a mutual respect and dialogue between us all.

With regard to the historical shows, we really wanted to open up the program early on, as the space is just perfect for it. It's something we're constantly trying to refine. Calder might have been slightly outside our realm, but it was an amazing opportunity and a fabulous show. Next November, for example, we will stage a retrospective of works by British Minimalist Bob Law, in partnership with Karsten Schubert. I hope this will bring people to recognize what a great artist he was. Also, there's a constant desire to invite outside curators to stage shows or projects in the gallery. I don't want the gallery to be a closed, self-reflective entity. I love these collaborations.

— You also have a film-club program. Who runs that, and how does it work?

That was really a one-off, the cine-club was a fantastic two-week project organized by curator Francesco Manacorda. The films were running in a temporary cardboard cinema built by Slovenian artist Tobias Putrih. One of my favorite moments of the gallery.

— Is there anything you can't stand about running a gallery?
Perhaps there are some things I can keep to myself.

— What advice would you give to a new collector of contemporary art?
Same old advice: Go for quality, never for status. Look and learn before you begin. Be ambitious. Take financial risks, and don't follow the pack.

— Some people say this crisis will make the art world better. What's your view?
I would like to think so. It's still too early to tell. In the past few years, we have seen extraordinary excess, particularly in London, without any critical endorsement. It would be great to see some of the old rules back: Auction houses should remain auction houses, galleries should remain galleries and not Kunsthalles, and collectors should remain collectors.

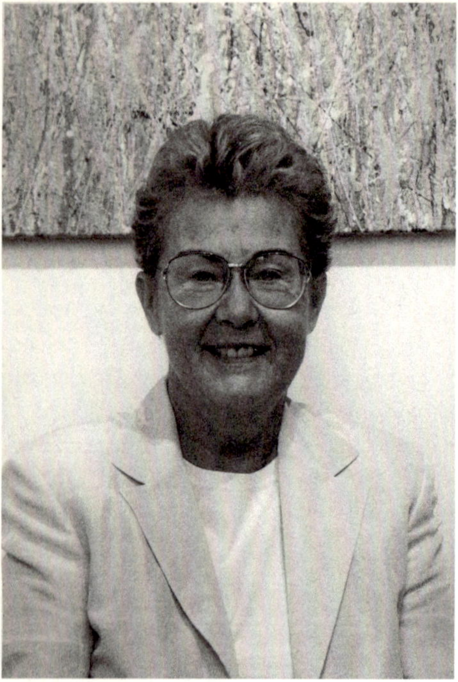

Helga de Alvear

Helga de Alvear

GALERÍA HELGA DE ALVEAR, MADRID

— Can you tell me briefly about your background?

I was born in Germany and came to Spain in 1957. I married a Spanish architect in Madrid, and in 1980, after having three daughters, I started working with Galeria Juana Mordó. In 1982, I became the proprietor of the gallery, but luckily, Juana lived until March 1984; she was the best teacher one could ask for. In 1995, when the gallery moved to a new location, I finally changed the name to my own.

— You are also a collector—you have one of the most impressive private contemporary art collections in Spain, with more than 2,000 works. How did you to start collecting? Do you think you've made mistakes as a collector?

I started my own collection in 1967, and, like any other self-taught person, I've made mistakes. Because in art, like most times in life, things are *sehen, verstehen, lieben*: see, know, desire.

— What acquisitions are you most proud of?
Always the last ones: Right now, it's Walid Raad/ Atlas Group, Ai Weiwei, and Santiago Sierra—a work from his latest show at MARCO (Museo de Arte Contemporánea) in Vigo.

— You have set up the Fundación Helga de Alvear and launching an art center in the city of Caceres, where your collection will be on permanent view. What is the center's mission?
It will be a private art center with a lot of possibilities for the region and Spain. It will hold my collection and will present shows and projects around it.

— What role can and should a contemporary art collector play with regard to society?
A collector makes his collection because he wants to, and I don't think he has to think about how it is used. Suddenly, the collection is so big that in the end it can help the culture. Personally. I like things given for public use.

— Let's talk about your work as a gallery owner. I imagine that running a gallery is far more complex than collecting. Are there are some aspects you don't like about the job? Are there things you'd happily do without?

I'm lucky to have lots of possibilities, so I can do just the shows I want in my gallery, not ones that I have to. Thanks to the gallery, I've learned a lot. It forces me to keep up to date with the art scene, so I could not do without it.

— What type of collector can you really not stand? Who are the ones that irritate you most?
Those who buy only by hearing and not by seeing.

— Do you have people you can rely on? Is it difficult to remain on top of things after forty years?
I had and still have a wonderful team to help me, and I hope they will always help me to get better.

— With all your experience, can you give some advice to a young person who wants to start collecting art today?
Sehen, verstehen, lieben.

Massimo De Carlo

GALLERIA MASSIMO DE CARLO, MILAN

— I've read that you started collecting art in your early twenties, before you became a gallery owner. Is that true?

Yes, it is. In 1982–83, I won a small sum of money on the football pools, and with the help of some friends who were interested in art, I decided to buy some works.

— You were a student studying pharmacology in those days. In an interview, you said that it was a rather unsuccessful debut. Why was that?

I bought some good-quality works of contemporary art, but somehow they didn't really represent me. It wasn't a failure, but objectively speaking, this foray into the world of art didn't help me in my work. Having said that, it was an interesting apprenticeship.

— In the light of this initial experience, what advice would you give to a young collector who has a bit of money to invest in art?
I would suggest he or she go to art fairs and galleries, and read magazines. And I would say don't buy anything immediately—let at least a year go by, so you can get a good idea before investing.

— Would you suggest they buy small works or start off immediately with something a bit more challenging?
After a year, they ought to understand what they're interested in, what their feelings are, and if their understanding allows them to join the so-called debate on contemporary art. They ought to buy works that somehow give them satisfaction, and that are part of the flow of life in the contemporary art system.

— We have all had some significant encounters in our lives. What were yours?
I come from the world of music, and everything I have learned has come from working with musicians. The person who somehow helped me form a set of values, which have also proved to be very useful in art, is the African-American pianist Muhal Richard Adams. He's still going strong, and he's fairly well known. Generally speaking, I'd say music has been my great master.

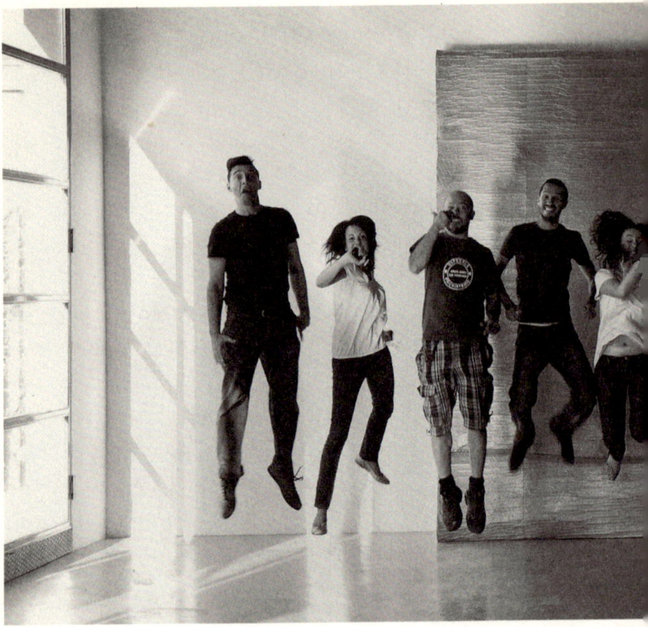

You know, in those days you were dealing with some extraordinary people, absolutely great artists in terms of their quality of thought. And yet there was very little cash around, there was just a desire to raise the quality of music. What's more, it was a very varied and rapidly evolving world. There was a lot of overlapping and a lot of integration—a sort of free exchange of creativity that got me thinking, and that really helped me interact with artists. When talking with artists, you need to talk their language.

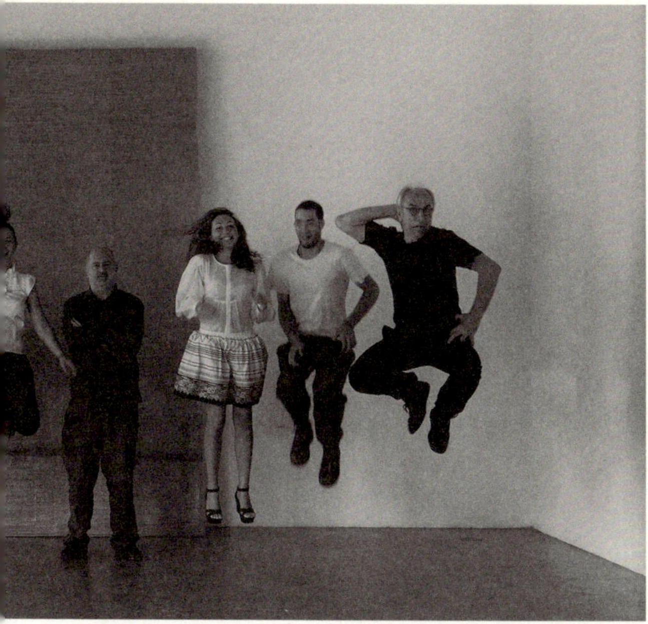

From left: Mauro Vignando, Francesca Valente, Cristhian Raimondi, Stefano Zicchieri, Elena Tavecchia, Oda Albera, Massimo De Carlo, Anna Maria Soverini, Manuel Scano, Manfred H. Teupen
Photo: Alessandro Zambianchi

The greatest failures in my work have come when I haven't been able to use the language of art with artists—the language of feelings and of passion for their work. In art, passion needs to come from within, not without. It's a special sort of drive—like a software application working alongside other mechanisms.

— Talking of special encounters, you started working in the art world with Piero Cavellini, the son of a rather singular personality.

Yes, Piero was the son of Guglielmo Achille Cavellini. The father was a great collector in the 1950s and '60s, but he decided to sell everything in order to support the greatest artist of the century: himself. A very curious character, full of inventiveness, and he did all sorts of interesting things. I've always followed Guglielmo Achille from a certain distance. Piero was more sensitive—a poet, and someone who perceived the lyrical aspects of art and of the art world, which in those days wasn't fully developed. He helped me a great deal in terms of developing my use of language.

— In those days you were also working as a pharmacist.

I worked as a pharmacist at night, and as Piero Cavellini's assistant during the day. This went on from 1985 to 1987, the year I opened my gallery. Even so, I carried on working as a pharmacist until 1989–90.

— What were you interested in when you opened your gallery?

I was mainly interested in artists who were associated with Neo-Geo. I worked with John Armleder, Olivier Mosset, and Steven Parrino, who formed part of a much wider world. In those days, there was a lot of talk about Peter Halley, Gerwald Rockenschaub, and people like Ashley Bickerton and Haim Steinbach, who came from the International With Monument gallery in New York's East Village.

— Jeff Koons had his first exhibition there. Were you already going to New York in the 1980s?
Yes. In September '87, for example, I met Steven Parrino in New York. My collaboration with Italian artists came later.

— But you did some interesting work with Italian artists, too. How did you meet Maurizio Cattelan, for example?
Maurizio used to come to my gallery. He had a rather oblique approach, one might say, to relationships: He would come in, say a couple of words, and then vanish. I met him in about '88 or '89. Actually, it was more he who pursued me rather than me pursuing him, and I must say that for a couple of years I didn't even take him that seriously. Then in 1991, I saw Renato Barilli's "Anninovanta" exhibition in Bologna. Maurizio was showing *Stadium*—an important work that is basically a very long table football game. I was very struck by it, and later that year we started working together.

— Then, in the mid-1990s, you also came across this group of guys who were living on Via Fiuggi in Milan: Diego Perrone, Giuseppe Gabellone, Simone Berti, and so on.

Yes, we were all living together. I came into contact with them because it was a particular moment in my life—I sort of changed my ideas and habits, especially at the personal level, and I was more drawn to spending my evenings and nights with others. They used to go to the gallery, and it was an inspiring relationship, although it was more social than artistic. In those days, the artists in the Via Fiuggi group were just emerging, but they had yet to develop a fully formed language. The "Avanblob" exhibition happened in 1990, bringing real stimulus and energy to the scene in Milan. Mario Airò, Liliana Moro, and Bernhard Rüdiger had come together in a sort of collective, even though they were all fiercely independent. In the end, only Airò and Moro became well established. This was very important at the emotional level, in terms of energy. Much more important than Via Fiuggi.

— That exhibition certainly played a role in the history of Italian art, moving away from the rather stagnant and self-referential painting scene in Rome.

Precisely. Even so, it had greater impact in terms of ideas than in terms of results.

— You once said in an interview that contemporary art collectors are fairly easy to influence, and they end up influencing each other. It was a curious concept.

What I meant was that they are easily influenced by the context. You can often see how collections are influenced by each other, even sometimes appearing like photocopies. On a personal level, the chances of me influencing a collector are pretty small. As gallery owners, we are seen simply as people who are trying to sell something. I hardly ever call collectors.

But the ideal, all-round gallery owner ought to be able to interact with both artists and collectors. I remember how in the late 1980s I had the good fortune to spend about an hour with Leo Castelli, when he still had his gallery on West Broadway, and he was still working with artists like Jasper Johns and Robert Rauschenberg. What really struck me was his extraordinary kindness and his ability to make people feel at ease. A gallery director needs to have a very open approach to relationships. He or she needs to have the ability to personalize relationships at whatever level. And this, unfortunately, is not a specialty of mine.

— Is there an artist with whom you enjoy a particularly intense relationship?

To be quite honest, I think I have that with all my artists, or, at least, with all those who've allowed me to come close enough, and whom I've seen often enough. Establishing human relationships with a person also means accepting a level of conflict. A relationship with anyone has its problematic moments.

— Would you continue to do this job if you couldn't have a dialogue with your artists?

You need to recognize that there are always time limits in this job, and the energy you put into relationships gets used up. I'm very glad I've been able to have a relationship with my artists, and I'm happy that I still have it, but this work inevitably evolves in directions that require a "non-consumption" of the person. And then, of course, artists take, ask, and absorb. The relationship between the artist and the outside world is always somewhat based on parasitism, on profit—it's in an artist's DNA. You have to be careful not to be worn down.

— You once told me that after your experience with the gallery, you'd like to start up something new. What would you like to do?

I like to think I would be able to take on other challenges. I don't know—writing, possibly, or opening a restaurant or something. Or even taking over a

small business and seeing if it's possible to turn it into something interesting. Art keeps your eyes wide open to the world, and in my twenty-two years in the field, I've built up a remarkable level of knowledge and experience that might be useful in other areas as well. Perhaps I could do something totally separate from art.
If I had to measure what I've done against what I would like to do, I could say that so far I really haven't done anything. I'm so anxious and hyper-critical that I never feel particularly satisfied. The number of things I can't do is endless. I spend a fair amount of my time thinking about all the things I haven't managed to do.

— That's curious. You're considered one of the most interesting European gallery owners!
Yes, but in the end there are still things I haven't been able to do in my work. I could have worked with a particular artist but didn't, I could have bought that work but failed to. These are details, just trivialities, really; I've had a truly extraordinary experience. On a professional level, however, there are still lots of things I aspire to.

— What should a collector never do?
It depends a lot on the moment. But certainly, singing one's own praises, boasting. That annoys me.

— You're also a gourmand. Is there a restaurant in Milan you'd like to suggest to our readers?
It's very hard to talk about a top-quality restaurant, because it's a place that always tries to impose an all-round experience on you. The most interesting thing is to need something at one o'clock and have it at two. I'd say the best restaurant is one that satisfies your needs in this sort of extreme way. Then there are some extraordinary, sublime gastronomic experiences, when they really keep their word.

— Like El Bulli.
I'm fascinated by the process that goes on behind the creation of something in a restaurant. I like what happens in the construction of food, in how the food reaches your table. What fascinates me most is the various links in the chain.

— On the subject of systems and their workings, what do you think of contemporary art museums?
We've reached a point where the concept of a museum is basically that of an indispensable place for cultural entertainment. So, unfortunately, it slavishly follows all the rules of cultural entertainment: When it creates a scandal, it's a patinated, rather middle-class form of scandal; when it expresses itself, it needs to think about

emergency exits. The curator ends up having to ward off the board of directors. I think you could say that the great era of museums started with Beaubourg in 1977.

So what did they create? On the one hand, a great focus on the phenomenon of contemporary art, helping bring about the rise of a more or less mindful, and excitable, form of collecting. On the other hand, on the level of ideas, it produced bureaucrats. No great contemporary art thinker has ever run a museum. Pontus Hultén contributed enormously, but because he was totally independent. Ideas and developments have generally gone to the fringes of the museum, not into its rooms. Museums have simply come up with low-level translations of ideas. In the best cases, a museum is to art what a great translator is to a writer. I find the situation of museums extraordinarily depressing right now.

— Are you saying this about the broader context, and not just Italy?

Yes, I'm talking about the planetary level. When I hear, "You know, we're going to be starting a contemporary art museum," it just makes me laugh, because as an institution, it's both a failure and outdated even before it gets off the ground.

In the past thirty years, museums have created a vision of contemporary art that, at its best, is agreeable or attractive. But they're useful in terms of circulating news and information.

— If you were Italy's minister of culture, and you were asked to invest funds in order to make the Italian art system more interesting, what would you do? Is there an alternative type of museum? The Kunsthalle, possibly?

No. I think that what is needed is an authentic long-term program. Building a museum itself takes four or five years, if all goes well. Contemporary art should be created by working in the territory, without having to build places. Then I would divide up the territory into local areas that each somehow has a life of its own and that produce events and create things, like small workshops. Then, inside these individual cells, in these small areas, I would introduce forms of competition and, thus, of evaluation. In terms of ideas, I would like someone to say something different from the others, and to say it better, and to say it in a more powerfully contemporary way, with a more forward-looking approach than what we find now. This would be a serious approach, but of course it isn't feasible—possibly in other countries that are more serious than Italy, for it always demands high levels of evaluation, judgment, and thought. I wouldn't start from an idea of art when doing this, but from an idea of the contemporary. For example, I'm not Catholic, so when someone says that the Vatican should have its own pavilion at the Biennale, I am personally enthusiastic. The more jarring the suggestion, the more interesting the difference between people's thoughts will be, and the greater the gap between one approach and another. The best ideas are the ones that come out of that gap.

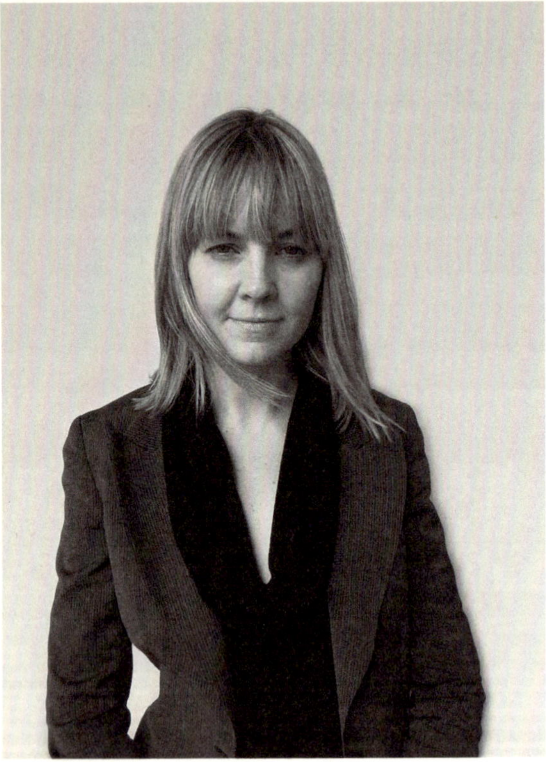

Elizabeth Dee

Elizabeth Dee

ELIZABETH DEE GALLERY, NEW YORK

— Let's start with your most recent project: In March 2009, you opened the nonprofit space X Initiative in Chelsea—whose advisory board I'm a member of—and it immediately attracted a great deal of attention. How did the idea come about?

I developed the concept of X Initiative during the economic crisis, to respond to what I foresee will be a very important, transitional time in the art world. What became apparent at the beginning of 2009 was that there was a renewed interest in rethinking the entire art system in a collective way. The possibility for radical changes was brought about by the economic situation, and I saw an opportunity to engage an expanded network in a variety of ways. We formed a nonprofit organization that would exist for twelve months, with a global group of advisors, and we have site programming and weekly events in the former Dia Center for the Arts on West 22nd Street. The very short lead times that we impose on ourselves, in order to keep the programming as relevant as possible, keeps the conversation very dynamic, participatory, and active.

X has finished its first and second round of exhibitions, which included a survey of Super-8 films by Derek Jarman; site-specific installations by Christian Holstad and Mika Tajima; and solo exhibitions by Luke Fowler, Tris Vonna-Michell, and Keren Cytter.

— As you just mentioned, X is in the building that was formerly occupied by Dia, one of the most interesting exhibition venues in Chelsea. I'd like to ask you a rather indiscreet question: Who's footing the bill? Who pays the rent and the production costs for the various projects?

The timing of the funding, the building's vacancy, and the willingness of the arts community could not ever be replicated, even if we had opened just a few months later. We have funding from a private foundation, a donated space from the building's owners, and the wonderful support and ideas of the international art world. When these three things happened together in tandem, we really had an opportunity.

— What was your educational background?

I made art and played music throughout my early life. It was something in me from the beginning. My family supported my interest in the arts, and I had some amazing educational opportunities that helped shape my interests. I went to Cranbrook Kingswood, which is a renowned high school outside Detroit and on the same campus as the Cranbrook Academy of Art. The schools were designed by Eliel Saarinen, and it was an unparalleled art environment. Afterward, I attended Mount Holyoke College, which is a women's college in Massachusetts, and studied art, art history, feminist studies, and philosophy. Many of my personal interests and educational background have found their way into my work today.

— In 2002, you opened your gallery in Chelsea. What had you been doing before then? Tell me about your previous experiences in the world of art.

When I graduated from college in the mid-1990s, the art world was coming out of a long recession, and jobs in the arts were few. There were not as many galleries, and the pace was much more gradual. I moved to San Francisco to intern at the San Francisco Cinematheque and then landed my first gallery job as a receptionist at Daniel Weinberg Gallery. Dan showed artists from his generation who emerged in the 1970s; when it first opened in 1975, the gallery was like a West Coast outpost of New York's Bykert Gallery. He represented Brice Marden, Sherrie Levine, Jeff Koons, Richard Artschwager, and Robert Mangold when they were emerging artists. Being able to experience that type of history twenty years later was a valuable experience for me. It was a very personal and connoisseur-based engagement, and Dan had a wonderfully intuitive curatorial style in the gallery.

I had thought of going to art school, but ultimately I decided to go to New York. I was twenty-three at the time. I had a number of jobs there and worked for a variety of dealers, programs, and artists. My last gallery job was as director of Luhring Augustine. After that I went out on my own. I was in my late twenties and still forming in many ways.

Before starting my current gallery, I did some experimental work in private spaces or semi-private collaborations. I've never been afraid to try new things or take risks, and I've always liked working with other people. I had a "by appointment" space in a Soho kitchen and would make big dinners to bring people together for a variety of conversations. Many people visited me there, from Jeff Koons to Jeffrey Deitch to European collectors who had heard about what I was doing by word of mouth. Working with unrepresented artists and historical works and positioning them in exhibition environments was how I learned to curate and form a program.

— In the seven years of your gallery thus far, you have put on the first solo shows of numerous artists who have become names today—the exhibitions of Adrian Piper, Alex Bag, Josephine Meckseper, Ryan Trecartin, and Mika Tajima/New Humans come to mind, to name just a few. How do you choose your artists? What struck you, for example, about the work of Ryan Trecartin the first time you saw it?

I'm interested in artists who engage in expanded practices, and this tends to often be manifested in the conceptual, political, and social areas. I have always searched for a more complex dialogue in the selection of artists for the gallery and am attracted to art that commands its own territory yet converses with its peers and can be discussed in potentially historical terms. We represent an intergenerational group of artists—having Renée Green, Adrian Piper, and Josephine Meckseper in the same gallery as younger artists like Meredyth Sparks, Mika Tajima/New Humans, Ryan Trecartin and Lizzie Fitch yields interesting associations and gives the gallery a point of view. We gave Ryan and Josephine their first solo exhibitions, but we have never just represented emerging artists. It was always very important from the beginning to develop an intergenerational program with connections between the artists represented, and to point to future conversations in art. We also reengaged with artists, realizing "comebacks" of mid-career and older artists like Alex Bag and Adrian Piper and Renée Green. We have always supported female artists and pre- and post-feminist dialogues within the history of conceptual art, so it made a great amount of sense.

The first work of Ryan's that I saw was the 2004 video *A Family Finds Entertainment*. I had never seen anything quite like it. It was entirely new, and I could barely wrap my mind around the speed and velocity of what I was witnessing. It blew me away. When I met him, I just knew that he was at the beginning of something that we had never seen before in video. His balance, intelligence, discipline, and vision were already concrete and very solid. We've just seen the start of what is possible from Ryan and others who will follow him.

— You opened your gallery at a time of great euphoria in the market. How are you dealing with the present crisis? You already talked about how it created the opportunity for the nonprofit X Initiative, but how is the economy affecting your commercial business?

There is no real way to deal with the crisis but to focus on survival. That means downsizing and identifying where the opportunities are and focusing exclusively on those parts of the gallery. It's a horrible time for the world, and I think that we have to be more creative with less. It will yield some interesting propositions and balance some inflation in the larger market, but we have to be disciplined and find new inspiration in this landscape.

— What are the encounters that have changed your life?

Any gallerist will say that her artists have had the most impact on her thinking, and I would certainly agree.

I am indebted to these artists, who not only inspire me through their work but also take part in conversations about our gallery and the choices that affect the gallery's identity. Gareth James and Eric Baudelaire have been the most influential; Gareth had a wide influence on the gallery's development at an early stage. Meredyth Sparks and Mika Tajima, two of our newest additions, have joined them in taking special interest in where the gallery is headed in the future. I have special friendships with them, and it is a fruitful dialogue.

— Can you give five good pieces of advice to a young person who wants to open an art gallery today?

1. Develop a program rather than selecting individual artists, and think about your gallery in the context of other galleries. What do you propose to contribute?
2. Build relationships in ways that are long term, and always resolve issues in ways that you can be proud of later on.
3. Keep costs low, even in good times, and try to save for the hard times—you will have many.
4. Always pay your artists first before paying yourself.
5. Remember, your track record and reputation are all you have; act accordingly.

Nicole Timonier

EVERGREENE, GENEVA

— Nicole, you opened your gallery in 2002, and you soon made a name for yourself as a talent scout. What was your educational background?

Actually, I had a relatively limited art background. In the mid-1990s, I started working with Rachel Lehmann Gallery in Lausanne. And one summer I worked at a gallery in East Hampton started by Rachel and Metro Pictures.

My experience was short, but the exposure to artists and artwork was quite vast: Jeff Koons, David Salle, Ross Bleckner, Meier Vaisman—those are just a few examples.

— When did you decide to become a gallery director?

When I returned to Switzerland after three years in New York, I wanted to capitalize on my own experience but preferred not to join any particular gallery, so I decided to open my own. It was a leap in the dark. I wandered around Geneva looking for an empty space, having only a vague idea of the dynamics of the local art scene.

— What were the greatest difficulties you had at the beginning?

Being invisible, then ignored.

— How did you put together your program? How do you choose your artists?

At first, the program was articulated around New York artists, consigning their works from established galleries in my personal network. Very quickly, I understood that the effort and cost were not proportionate to the potential market in Geneva, so I started looking for other artists. It was at this moment that the building where my gallery was—at the time, called Greene Gallery—burnt down completely. After finding a new space, and sort of rising up from the ashes, I called it Evergreene.

By then my exposure to and interest in Swiss artists was growing stronger. I thought that the timing was perfect to re-create the gallery's reputation.

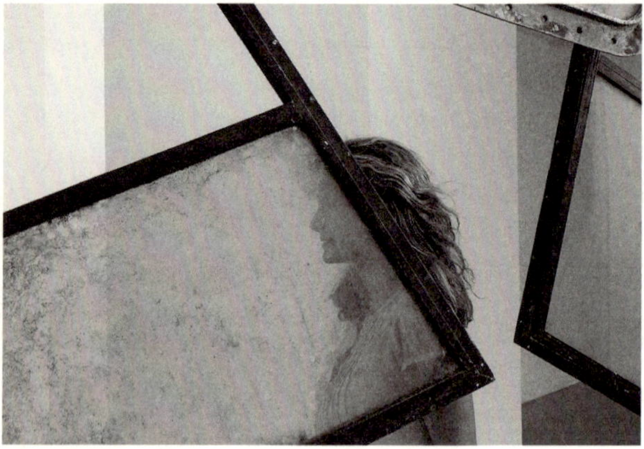

Nicole Timonier
Photo: Annik Wetter

At the time, there was a strong scene of Swiss artists who had no representation in Geneva, so Evergreene offered them their first opportunities: artists such as Jérémie Gindre, Frédéric Post, Valentin Carron, Pierre Vadi, Didier Rittener, and Andreas Dobler. Evergreene's program was built with guidance from local art institutions and, of course, from the artists themselves.

— What is Evergreene's relationship with the art schools in Lausanne and Geneva, and with museums and other institutions in Switzerland?

The art schools and institutions understood what we were doing right away and recognized that Evergreene was, in fact, trying to continue and complement their effort by offering a commercial environment, and we continue to enjoy excellent relationships with Switzerland's main art institutions today.

There was a certain amount of confidence in the art scene, which further encouraged us to continue working in this direction and discover the energy that exists in our own backyard. Unfortunately, I cannot say the same for some art critics who write in our local newspapers, as they appear to be totally uninterested and lack any real knowledge of contemporary art, especially of the scene here in Geneva.

— Do you think that the various elements in the contemporary art world in Switzerland manage to work together as a system? Do you notice differences in other countries?

I feel fortunate to have ended up in Switzerland and to have chosen this niche in the art world. For such a small country, Switzerland nurtures so many young artists, and many of them have recently reached an international platform. The art scene here also benefits from a constant dialogue between collectors, institutions, galleries, and artists. There's also a paradox within Switzerland's cultural scene: The country appears to be very tight and organized both socially and politically, but there is a strong undercurrent that creates tension, and out of this comes excellent talent.

— That's interesting. Can you tell me something more about this cultural undercurrent?

This undercurrent comes from the several alternative spaces run by serious curators and artists. For example, in the Romandy region, there's Circuit, in Lausanne, and a number of spaces in Geneva, such as Centre d'édition contemporaine, Forde, Ecart, and Attitudes.

— When did you start working with Samuel Gross, the gallery's art director?

In 2007, Evergreene's lease ended, and the gallery came to a crossroads. Samuel Gross, who had worked the previous three years at Mamco (Musée d'art moderne et contemporain), in Geneva, as director Christian Bernard's assistant, came to the gallery and proposed to help expand Evergreene's program. Through Samuel's cultural and institutional background, he understood and respected the gallery's history, so he enriched the program with artists he calls "the family." Samuel co-curated Evergreene's last exhibition in our old space with the nonprofit Hard Hat. It was a group show of young talents, including Denis Savary, Guillaume Pilet, and Marta Rikiner-Radich, among others. In 2008, we opened our new space with Swiss artist Renée Levi. Since then, Samuel, who has a historical vision, has organized exhibitions of works by deceased artists Tony Morgan and Aldo Walker, and by foreign artists such as American artist Blair Thurman and Delphine Coindet, from France. Evergreene continues to support established Swiss artists, such as Andreas Dobler, Christian Robert-Tissot, and Pierre Vadi, and we always keep our sights on Evergreene's main direction, showing young Swiss artists like Denis Savary, David Hominal, Damien Navarro, and Emilie Ding.

— How are you dealing with the current economic crisis? Do you think this crisis might lead to improvements in the art system?

Evergreene took on higher costs just before the crisis. The timing was bad, and the risks continue to be high. However, it is my belief that if we can survive the storm, we will find ourselves in a more transparent and sincere art environment. Positioned as it is, Evergreene may have a unique opportunity to promote its values and its views.

— What needs to change in the art world?

My answer to this question isn't very original, but the art world has become saturated; we need less quantity and more quality. It's not unfair to state that to be a good gallerist, artist, or collector, you need at least a minimum of education or experience. Someone coming to a contemporary art exhibition should be challenged and introduced to new concepts, not just a new trend.

— What is art for?

There is a difference between the art world and art; my opinion on the art world is to some extent answered above, but art exists on so many levels—art really is for everyone.

Jean-Claude Freymond-Guth

FREYMOND-GUTH & CO FINE ARTS, ZURICH

— The first place you opened was a nonprofit, Les Complices, in 2002, when you were still a student. In 2006, your last academic year, you and a group of artists decided to transform this project into a commercial gallery. You're also an artist and a curator. Does the gallery allow you to work on your different interests? Isn't Jean-Claude the artist constantly besieged by Freymond-Guth the gallery owner?

When I decided to open a gallery together with some of the artists we worked with at Les Complices, I did make a clear decision not to pursue a career as an artist or, at least, definitely not within a common understanding of authorship. I do believe that my experience as an artist as well as a curator helps to establish an interesting, multilayered, and yet commercial environment that goes further than being a hip boutique. Also, I guess that a certain lack of

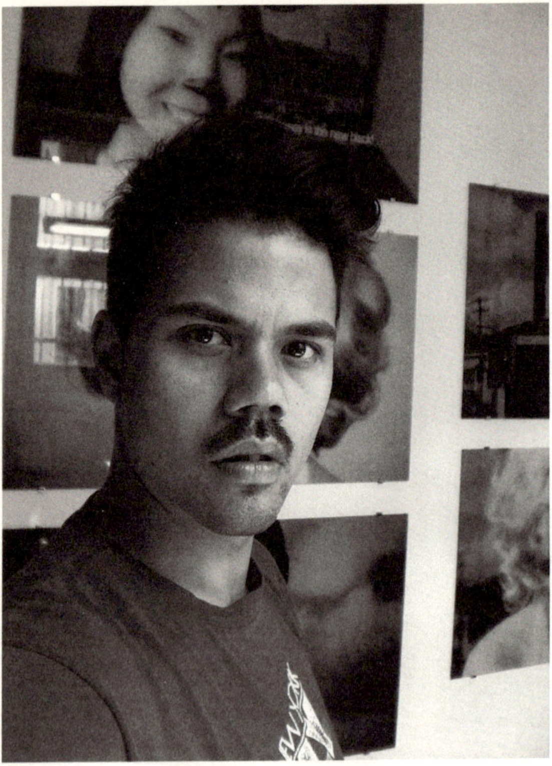

Jean-Claude Freymond-Guth

knowledge about the systematics of galleries and the art market in general were more protective than harmful. Even if "success" might not be as quick this way, I do believe in an organic growth of things, and the authenticity that comes from that does count for a lot, especially in these difficult times.

— I read in an interview that you moved from Berlin to Zurich for personal and study reasons. How were you greeted in the city? Was there acceptance of and interest in your project?
It all was very welcoming, and people were curious about this new kid in town. Certainly there was skepticism, but mainly from the side of the art school and its jealous teachers.

— You also work a lot as a curator. I imagine that not all the artists you invite to your various curatorial projects are also of interest to you as a gallery owner. How do you choose the artists you work with in the gallery?
I think if I had more capacities I would definitely also include more of those artists into the gallery program. The interesting difference, though, lies in the short and intense time and precise content. One works with artists on defined curatorial projects, and not all of those have the same quality in a long-term relationship.

— In 2006, you and another three artists set up Kunsthaus Perla-Mode. What is that project?
It is the temporary use of an old building in Zurich's red-light district that I initiated, together with several individuals of diverse curatorial, artistic, and publishing backgrounds, as a space of dialogue between commercial and non-commercial, improvised and long-term research projects. It also functions as a lively social environment. I find that in a city like Zurich there is a great need for the improvised and the temporary, not necessarily destined to lead to commercial success. While my gallery moved on to a permanent space down the street last fall, needing a safer structure, Perla-Mode continues to be unique in its diversity and numerous activities.

— How are you dealing with the present crisis? Many curators and critics, but also some gallery owners, say that it came at the right time, and that there was almost a need for it.
Working with artists who are rather unknown internationally and who often adopt experimental and process-oriented practices, I definitely profit from the general reduction of speed in how careers and markets are being built. These are tough times nevertheless.

— What was your best intuitive decision, and what mistake do you wish you'd never made?

I am very influenced by my vivid intuition in general, so it has led to many smaller and greater successes and mistakes. But I am happy to see that some artists that I work with are now getting the recognition they deserve, when nobody had heard of them or knew about their potential when I first met them. If I started again, I would probably reduce my activities to fewer and more focused.

— Is there something you can't stand or that you don't like about your job as a gallery owner?
I have great trouble dealing with people who are over-ambitious, and/or who are more interested in power and status than anything else. And there are quite a few of those in the art world.

— Who do you think the best collectors are? And the worst?
My experience so far has showed me that the best collectors are often the most modest, genuine, interested people, who at first sight would never reveal all their monetary, social, or intellectual influence. The opposite, I find, are the worst.

— Let me ask Jean-Claude the curator a question. There are some people who say that the days of the great historic festivals, like the Venice Biennale, Documenta, and even Manifesta, are over and that

they've lost their appeal. What do you think? If you were asked to curate one, would you?

Personally, I've always become very quickly tired of events without content, and I find parties with my friends are often more fun than with the international art world–hoppers. But anything that goes beyond the sometimes very shallow spectacle of past years, without being elitist, is definitely extremely important for a continuous discourse, and I would be honored to participate in it.

Nathalie Boutin and Solène Guillier

GB AGENCY, PARIS

— What is gb agency?

For us, a gallery is a place where ideas come together in the form of exhibitions—it's a meeting place where interaction can take place, where it is possible to share and discover. Gb agency has always wished to contextualize and explain, out of respect for the artists and the public. Opening the gallery with works from the 1960s by Robert Breer, for example, implied a desire to share a work of memory. We wanted to make this magnificent and disconcerting work known. It had never really been fully understood during the years of Minimalism and Conceptual art because its mixture of experimental cinema and moving sculpture didn't fit into the standard formats of those years. This meant that his work couldn't be included in a straightforward, linear history of art like that of the past fifty years—there was no room for this unstable, doubt-filled work.

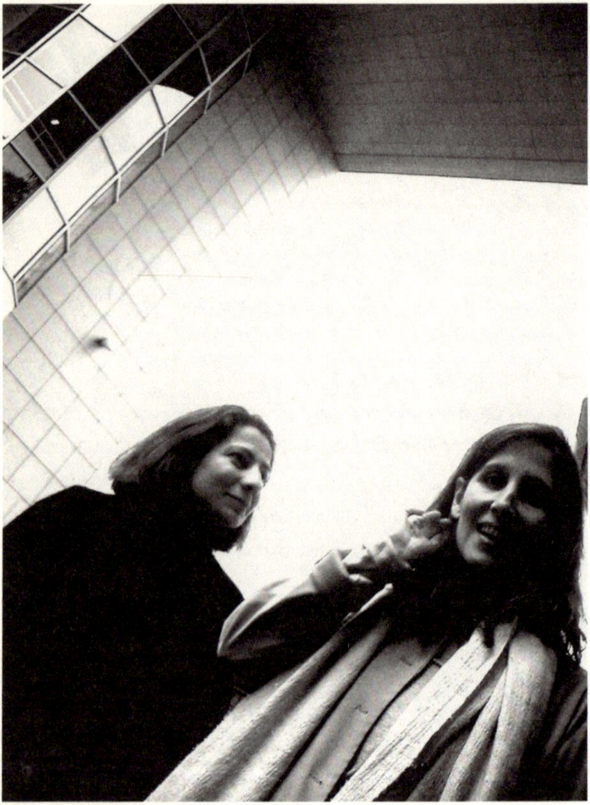

Solène Guillier / Nathalie Boutin

Early on, gb agency also started working toward a new interpretation of artists from the former Soviet bloc, reconsidering a period in the history of art that we all had very poor knowledge of. And we also continued our studies of different cultures, like that of Thailand, which plunged us into different forms of interpretation, and other notions. This work of discovery and rediscovery is an enormous pleasure for us.

— What is The Fair Gallery?

The Fair Gallery emerged from a feeling of great unease. This came out one evening during a get-together with friends: We all felt we wanted to create something that could react to and overcome the long-established mechanisms of the art-fair world. The Fair Gallery brought together the galleries Raster (Poland), Jan Mot (Belgium), Hollybush Gardens (UK), and gb agency, and it will continue its work with other members, and other future forms. The Fair Gallery's main activity is to represent participating galleries at art fairs in the form of an exhibition, experimenting with the potential and limits of a new format: The Fair Gallery doesn't exist physically as a real space but is activated with each fair project.

— It strikes me that gb agency is further proof of the hybridization of roles in contemporary art world. There's a tendency to reinterpret the old, established

"trades," in a new way. For example, I spent four years in New York as the US editor of *Flash Art* before becoming the director of Artissima, a contemporary art fair. Samuel Keller, who is neither an art critic nor a curator, was asked to direct the Beyeler Foundation after having run Art Basel. Critics, artists, and gallery owners have now become curators, and curators become artists or even gallery directors, while collectors tend to become the directors of their own foundations (although they would rather run museums). What's going on in the art world? How do you interpret all this?

At the moment, there's a certain degree of permeability between the various sectors and roles in the world of contemporary art. When the gallery opened in 2001, gb agency created a program with an unusual vision. This called both for a curatorial project each year within an institution, and for three solo exhibitions and a group exhibition in the form of research within the gallery premises. Generally speaking, this reluctance to give ourselves an identity, and this need to eliminate the barriers within our activity, certainly has to do with a new way of discovering the world today. Access to knowledge is currently instantaneous and all-encompassing for everyone. Discovering an artist allows us to discover other universes at the same time. As a result, we need to invent new points of view, and new relationships between individuals.

While what we see depends on where we are, our angle of vision ought to open up 360 degrees. After Catherine David's Documenta in 1997, art—which had been at a standstill, with linear canons—burst out into new ways of thinking and associating, with temporal deviations and with an eye on parallel forms of knowledge.

To come back to the actual organization of these "hybrid galleries," we also need to think about such things as the Foksal Foundation or the Raster gallery in Poland, Gregor Podnar's experience in Slovenia, Kurimanzutto's in Mexico, or that of Vitamin Creative Space in China. Via their own invented methods, and in the face of widespread ignorance of their own local art history, they've all had to reinterpret this history while also encouraging contemporary work. They have chosen the gallery model as a solution—and thus a commercial solution, even though hybrid—in order to improve their position and visibility on the international scene. This has helped give them a market.

Another example of hybridization is the X Initiative in New York. It is examining all these various different roles, without ever letting them conflict. The advisory board consists of institutions, gallery directors, artists, historians, critics, and curators—we are on the board, as are you—and we all spend a year working together.

In our opinion, this is an excellent platform, because it highlights the need to bring together ideas, action, and energy.

— Yes, I agree. My education was in art, history, and philosophy. What is your background?
We both studied the history of art in the classic sense of the term (École du Louvre and the Sorbonne), and we were lucky to have professors who were very demanding in their vision of art. Later on, although rather by chance, we both ended up working in art galleries. Neither of us had thought of being gallery owners, but this apprenticeship helped change some of our ideas and made us realize the importance of a gallery's role.

— I have the feeling, though, that you're trying to question what that role really is. Basically, you're following on from what Air de Paris has done.
Air de Paris is important for us, because if we hadn't thought of becoming gallery owners, one possible solution for us might have been precisely Air de Paris—their commitment and their choices, their positions (which weren't intended as positions), their approach, which is neither formal nor dogmatic but very open-ended. What they showed us is that a gallery can be totally free in adopting an approach of its own. This freedom gave us immense energy.

We do, of course, constantly bring our role into question, and the fact that we're representing artists who invent forms and build possible models obliges us to be pretty demanding. As a result, we keep asking ourselves about this profession, its role, and the way it appears and is conveyed. The artists we work with are well aware that we can push the limits well beyond those of the gallery. Because art itself is a constantly evolving concept, we feel it is only right that the very structure of the gallery should try out and experiment with different forms and approaches, in the ways it exhibits and takes part in art fairs, and in its relationships with the public.

— Perhaps the term *art gallery* has become too limiting. Are you attempting to invent a more open form?
We've been trying to imagine a new form of gallery for the past eight years. It would be pretentious and presumptuous, however, to say that we've already gotten there. But we've paved the way for change in this profession, and all the potential this may bring. The gallery is a living organism, constantly interacting with artists and the public. In a certain sense, it's a world that has no rules, and that can dream its own dreams and create its own priorities. What needs to be done is to help production, spread ideas, and make it possible for works to last for a long time. But there's

also a need to create a balance in order to have the right conditions for taking on risks, remunerating these activities and generating income so that artists and their families can live. This is our "definition" of a gallery, but there are undoubtedly many others.

— I was struck by some of your interviews in which you talked of the "ethical" role of the gallery owner. It's curious to hear talk of ethics in a market context.
The way we see it, being ethical means absolute integrity in our relationships with the artist, the artwork, and the public. There's certainly no sort of moral judgment in it. We have nothing to hide: We're a commercial organization, and we do indeed have a relationship with the market, but we always try to make sure that the market has no influence on our decisions, and we always attempt to steer clear of anything based on its effects. It's a matter of being vigilant and maintaining a clear mind each and every day, and adopting a long-term vision.
Even though it's not always clear to distinguish, we attempt to create constant interaction between ideas and the way they're received. To be quite clear: We form a link between the artists and their works, between curators and their research, between collectors and their desires, between museum directors and their questions about collections, and between the public and its interest in art.

The gallery is open to everyone, and it is based on dialogue and mediation. We must be very demanding in everything we do, both in terms of the work we promote and in terms of helping it to be understood—this is true at an art fair and during a visit by a group of schoolchildren.
Being ethical for us also means keeping to our principles and not giving in to cynicism. It means believing in the interactions between art and life. If every aspect is clarified, it's easier to be ethical in a market context as well.

— What do you hate most about the art world? And what, on the contrary, inspires you the most?
Its forgetfulness, possibly, and the superficiality of some people's ideas.
Meeting up with artists and exhibition curators all the time—laughing and changing the world. Dreaming and letting others dream, inventing and sharing.

— What advice do you have for an aspiring gallery owner?
Never accept compromises. A gallery is an alchemical combination of form and content, space and ideas: Never separate them out. Work with artists who have a wealth of humanity. Don't give in to the pressures of time, to the effects of fashions; take your time and remain apart.

José Mário Brandão

GALERIA GRAÇA BRANDÃO, OPORTO/LISBON

— Before running the Graça Brandão gallery, you were the director of the Galeria Canvas in Oporto, until 1996. What was your background?
Secondary studies, a love for theater, *La Locandiera*, Carlo Goldoni, Ruggero Jacobbi . . .

— What are your main interests? How do you choose the artists for your gallery?
First of all, I work only with people I like. But I only work with them if they have good work. If not, they continue to be my friends, but I don't work with them. Albuquerque Mendes, Pedro Tudela, Rui Chafes, Orla Barry and Glen Rubsamen, João Tabarra, João Maria Gusmão + Pedro Paiva, João Galrão, Nelson Leirner, and, of course, Lygia Pape.

— Would you say there is an authentic contemporary art system in Oporto? What more do you think the city needs?
No, but you can speak about the Architecture School of Oporto, Fernando Távora, Siza Vieira, Eduardo Souto de Moura . . .

— What percentage of your gallery's turnover comes from local collectors, and how much do you depend on international art fairs?
We are living a special moment. The separation of the waters . . . Institutions have stopped purchasing. At the moment, lawyers and physicians are the ones that can buy works, and you understand why.

— Is there anything you don't like about the work of a gallery owner? Something you'd be quite happy to do without?
I like my gallery, I like my work, I like the kind of gallerist I am. I don't have a shop to sell paintings, pictures, sculptures . . . I have a gallery. You must understand what a gallery is, and in a small country, galleries have done important work.

— Many people say the present crisis is going to change the art system. What's your opinion?
Yes, yes, I hope so . . . the separation of the waters.

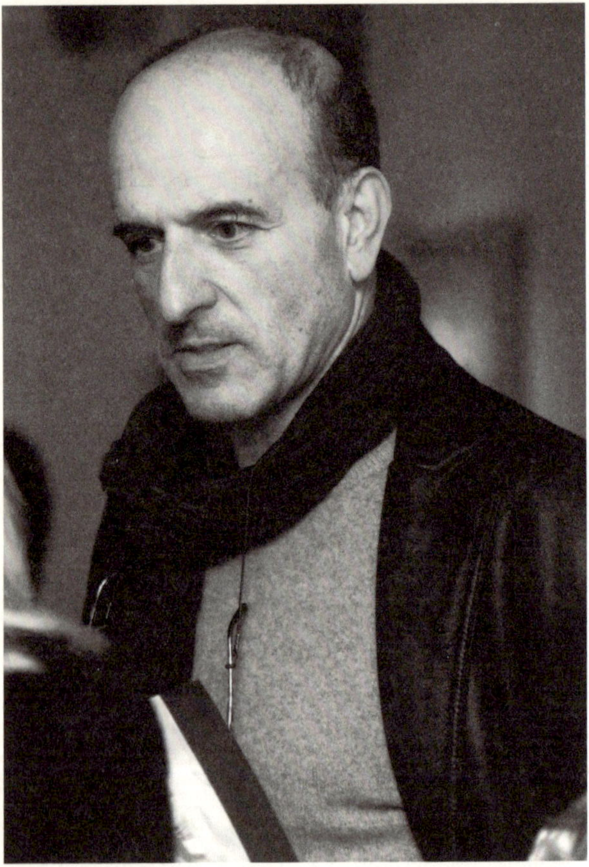

José Mário Brandão

— What do you think ought to change in the art world, and what, on the contrary, should always stay the same?
There are many ways to work in the art world. There is "spectacle art" and there is "real art." I prefer "real art," but I respect the other one.

— How is working in contemporary art in Portugal?
We live in a small country. We are used to saying that we are peripheral. That isn't true. We found new worlds. At this moment, we have very good Portuguese artists. Unfortunately, politicians—socialists or social democrats—don't promote Portuguese culture and language. Today, Portuguese is spoken in Europe, Africa, America, Asia, and Oceania. Before, you had to leave Portugal to be respected. Vieira da Silva went to Paris, when Paris was the right place. Paula Rego went to London, when London was the right place. Now you don't need to go to another country, because it's so easy to cross their borders. We live in a global world. Rui Chafes, Julião Sarmento, Pedro Cabrita Reis, and João Maria Gusmão + Pedro Paiva don't need to go away to have a place in the art world.

— In 2006, you opened new premises in Lisbon, while continuing with the gallery in Oporto. Is there a difference between the programs of the two galleries? How are the two cities different?

In 2000, Oporto was the European Capital of Culture, the center of art in Portugal. The Serralves Museum continues to be the most important museum of contemporary art, but for political reasons Oporto has lost its power, and now the art world comes to Lisbon. But when they come to my gallery I always have a bottle of Port to remind them that there are other important towns in Portugal. As Arthur Bispo do Rosário—a Brazilian artist, who received a holy message to make art—said, “I don’t like to do this, but I must.” In another words, I like Oporto, but I must stay in Lisbon, in order to promote my artists. The programs of the two galleries are not different. Portuguese collectors buy works all over the world. We Portuguese have always been driven to cross our borders. We created globalization.

— What advice would you give to a young collector who is approaching the contemporary art world today?
Visit galleries and museums, read books (not only on art), and trust honest people, who fortunately still exist in the art world.

Carol Greene

GREENE NAFTALI GALLERY, NEW YORK

— How did you get started? Where did you study, and what brought you to New York?

I studied art history and biology at Harvard, in Cambridge, Massachusetts, and I moved to New York after graduating in 1987, because I understood this to be the center of the art world. New York then was heady and extremely exciting. The markets had crashed, but the excess of the '80s was still in play. There was a kind of "last party" feeling to everything, and people were experimenting in all kinds of ways, which made New York feel so recklessly creative. I gravitated toward the unconventionality of the city. The art world was at the center of this cultural crossover of music and literature and dance, and the nightclubs were a vital part of a social exchange.

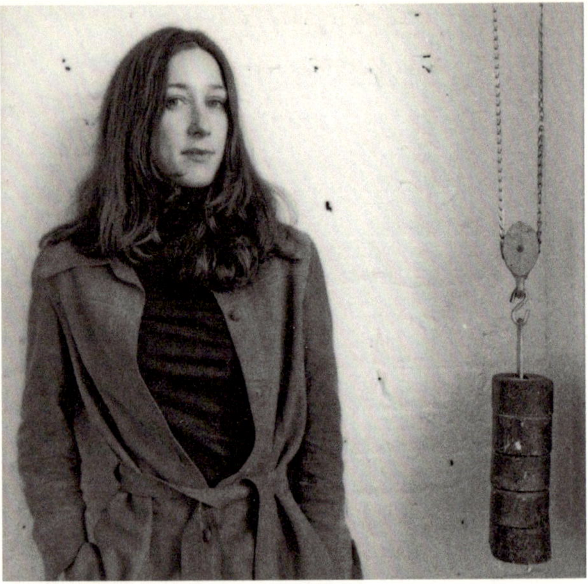

Carol Greene

So many people were going out, I was seeing art all the time, and everyone was accessible, including famous artists like Robert Rauschenberg and Francesco Clemente. I went to hundreds of studios and had great conversations, which started to shape my artistic consciousness.

I worked at the John Good Gallery, and John gave me a lot of freedom. I organized my first show, "Semi-Objects," at his gallery. It featured Katharina Fritsch in her New York gallery debut, a re-creation of Mike Kelley's chicken coop from the late '70s, and a fashion designer I loved named Christian Francis Roth. I also organized music and poetry events at the Thread Waxing Space in Soho. I was extremely excited about everything going on around me.

— In 1995, you opened your gallery in Chelsea, on Twenty-sixth Street, with Gloria Naftali. If I'm not mistaken, you were the first to open in that part of Chelsea. What are your memories of that time? What was the area like?

Opening in Chelsea in 1995 felt very edgy—literally being on the edge of Manhattan. I had started looking for a space that February. It was snowing all the time, freezing cold with bone-chilling wind whipping off the Hudson River. All of those large industrial warehouse blocks were particularly formidable, because there was almost nothing else around except a truck-stop

diner called Matty's, a bodega/betting joint on Tenth Avenue, and the gas station. I loved the desolate feeling of it, and the large beautiful open spaces.
I was very romantic about what I was trying to do. I felt as if I could pioneer an artistic movement of my generation, in a neighborhood that had a promise of its own. I was inspired by the austere beauty of the Dia Center for the Arts space and its rigorous programming, and I wasn't concerned at all that almost no one else was there. I thought, "If I show great art, everyone will come." We used to joke that there was a moat on Twenthy-third Street that people didn't want to cross, but after a few years it started to change. I was fortunate enough to meet Gloria and Raymond Naftali, who owned the building in which I wanted to rent a space and had a similar vision, and one thing led to another.

— There wasn't much money around in those days, but they were interesting times, and the New York art scene was changing rapidly. What was the life of a gallery owner like then compared with now?
There may not have been much money around, but capital takes many forms. We had such interesting lives, and we were all pursuing our ideas of the artistic life with total abandon. Money was the last thing we cared about, and I remember the artists were living on rice and beans, and my critic friends were on the ramen diet. It was definitely a rock-'n'-roll mentality.

We didn't think much about anything except doing what we wanted to do in a creative way. There was more focus on the art and the ideas. Our mentors at that time were Colin de Land and Pat Hearn. Anyone interested in contemporary art of the next generation was watching them, and they had this incredible style and intelligence that wasn't about money. I worked all the time, but I didn't think of it like that. I also went out all the time, and the transition from working to partying was seamless. I was doing exactly what I wanted to do all the time, during the day and the night.

— What do you think about the present financial crisis? Do you agree with those who say it will lead to positive changes in the art system?
I try not to think too much about the crisis and prefer to keep the focus on art. When the market was booming, did it affect artistic production? I'm sure it did, and perhaps it drew the wrong kind of people to this pursuit, but in the end, good art has a way of finding its place in the world. I do believe in this community and its ability to reinvent itself.

— You've always put on interesting group exhibitions, sometimes with artists not represented by the gallery—such as "Free Coke," in 1999, with Mary Heilmann, Chris Ofili, Jack Pierson, Piotr Uklanski, and others. Do you see yourself as a curator in addition to a gallery owner?

I take my job seriously and realize that I am running a commercial business and need to be responsible to that, but my primary motives are exhibiting work that moves me and has some kind of relevance to context.

— You're something of a talent scout: You put on the first exhibitions of works by Rachel Harrison, Laura Owens, and Paul Chan, among others. How did you meet Paul and decide to work with him, when he was practically unknown?

I showed Laura Owens's first painting in New York in a group show. Cameron Jamie and Mark Bradford also debuted in group shows at Greene Naftali. I offered Luc Tuymans his first solo show in New York when I was at John Good. Mark Manders and Jonathan Horowitz did solo shows at my gallery, as did Blake Rayne and Scott Lyall, although I no longer show them.

The way I was introduced to Paul is rather unusual. I ran into an artist at LAX, who was coming off a plane from a bongo-drumming festival in Hawaii. She mentioned that at Bard College she had taught one of the best artists ever to come through the program. It was like déjà vu—I'd heard that once before, and the artist turned out to be Matthew Barney. So I got his e-mail, arranged a meeting, and the rest is history.

It is very easy for me to show work that I believe in. I don't worry about its selling status, and so on, because I've always felt that success will come to work that deserves it. It was apparent to me how exceptional Paul was, and it was very lucky that he had such immediate success and recognition. The gallery has always had strong critical and curatorial support, which means a great deal to me—much more than showing brand names.

— What do you hate most about your job as a gallery owner? Is there one aspect of your profession that you'd willingly do without?
I tend to think of the things I love and make the rest bearable by not perceiving of them as negative . . .

— What are the encounters that have changed your life? Who has really influenced your way of thinking about art and looking at art?
This question is difficult for me—there have been a lot of people and art experiences that have inspired me along the way. To name a few, I would mention John Coplans, Alanna Heiss, Ileana Sonnabend, Leo Castelli, Pat Hearn, Marian Goodman, Colin de Land, Merce Cunningham, Alexander Schroeder, Jay Sanders, Alexander Rower, and Anne Pontégnie. Of course, the artists inspire you more than anyone. I can recommend a book that I found very helpful that came out in the '80s: *The Art Dealers*, by Laura de Coppet and Alan Jones. I also should not forget to mention Paula Cooper, who gave me the

single most important piece of advice when I was opening my gallery: “Get as much space as you can and you will figure out what to do with it later.”

— What would you have liked to do if you hadn’t become a gallery owner? Do you have other great interests?
I seriously considered becoming a surgeon or an oceanographer.

— One last question: What advice would you give to a young person who wants to open a gallery today?
Low overhead. If you’re going to create a strong artistic program, you need the mental freedom that comes from not being constrained by financial burdens.

Michael Lieberman and Jessie Washburne-Harris

HARRIS LIEBERMAN, NEW YORK

— Jessie, in the past you were the director of Friedrich Petzel Gallery, and you, Michael, were the director of Lombard-Freid Projects. If I'm not mistaken, you'd already met some time before, when you were both working at Gagosian. What did you learn from Larry? Is there anything you don't like about that style of gallery?

We met working at Gagosian on Madison Avenue in 1999. At that time, it was a much smaller operation, which meant we got to see all aspects of the business and how a high-level gallery operates. Larry is an incredible businessman and has an amazing eye for the best artworks. He demands professionalism and excellence from everyone who works for him, and we have tried to carry those standards with us over the last ten years.

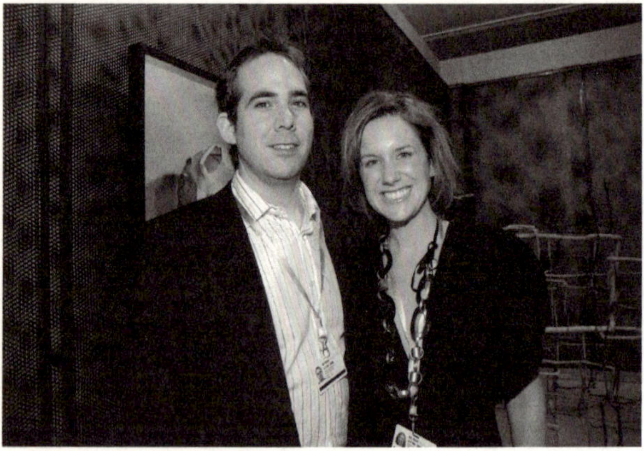

Michael Lieberman / Jessie Washburne-Harris

On the downside, Gagosian is probably the most obvious example of the emergence of the mega-gallery which we think is not so interesting at this moment. At a certain point, a gallery becomes so big that it is hard for all of the artists to stand out in the program. For the younger artists in these galleries, the model seems based more on a response to short-term financial considerations rather than long-term career development. Ultimately, we think most young artists don't benefit from this scenario. We are much more interested in developing relationships with our colleagues in other parts of the world and collaborating to use our combined experience and relationships to promote young artists.

— In 2005, you opened your own gallery on Vandam Street, and you made a name for yourselves with your interesting and sophisticated program. How do you choose your artists?
We were lucky to have almost two years to think about the kind of gallery we wanted to open. Most of this time was spent traveling, doing studio visits, reading, and talking to other people whose opinions we trust. We had a fairly good idea of the artists that we wanted to show. We were pleasantly surprised that almost all of them said yes, and we ended up opening the gallery with twelve artists.

— It's just four years since the gallery opened, and we're in the midst of a financial crisis. How are you reacting to this? How far are sales down from last year?
It was particularly difficult timing for us as we hadn't the chance to build a financial cushion, as had many peers who have been in business longer. The third year for us, as it is for most new businesses, was a real turning point. We have drastically reduced expenses while trying not to sacrifice the quality and ambition of the exhibitions that we mount. The two major downsides for us have been that we have less money to help artists produce work, and we cannot travel as much. However, we have learned how to use our money in a much smarter and more efficient way, and ironically, a lot of productive, creative solutions have come out of financial necessity.

— Some people say that, all things considered, the crisis is good for the art world.
It's a difficult thing. The size of the market led to a lot of mediocrity, so it's not necessarily a bad thing for there to be a weeding-out process. However, there is real pain involved in this, and unfortunately, it won't be the case that only the mediocre galleries or artists fail. We see the consequences every day in New York. As galleries go out of business, people are losing their jobs, fewer artists are able to support themselves with sales of their works, and storefronts sit empty.

We also see that the last decade of prosperity in the art world brought with it a lot of laziness. It was easy to throw money at production, museum exhibitions, gallery shows, everything. To continue to mount shows that matter, gallerists, artists, and museum curators all have to be a lot more creative. That, in the end, will probably bring about a lot of exciting changes and determine who will survive.

— Who is buying art at the moment in New York? I imagine that professionals, those with regular salaries, are still collecting. Which do you think is more solid at the moment, the European market or the American?
Yes, generally speaking young professionals have continued to collect works at lower price points. One good thing to have come out of the slowdown in activity is that there are more opportunities for museums. We have had a number of sales to fantastic institutions in the past six months. In the last month, we have noticed that some of the larger American collectors, who seemed to have taken a break from collecting last fall and winter, are now returning to the market. While we still do most of our business with American collectors, it does seem that the average European collector has been less affected by the financial volatility of the past year.

— How has the behavior of American collectors changed? Are they asking for more discounts?
One surprise has been that foot traffic in the gallery is down. Collectors seem to be looking at art less. In this market, everyone is looking for value, but for the most part our clients have been fairly respectful about discounts.

— Is there anything that you honestly can't stand about your job? Something you'd happily do without?
Saying no.

— Can you give some advice to a young person who wants to open a gallery in New York right now?
This is a fantastic time to open a gallery because there is a lot of openness to different models, and even if you want to open a more traditional space, the cost of entry is much lower. First and foremost, look at as much art as possible and read as much as possible; be aware of art being made globally as well as where you live. Make money before you spend it; start small but support your artists in a way that makes them think big.

Lisa Panting and Malin Ståhl

HOLLYBUSH GARDENS, LONDON

— What is your background? What sort of education and training did you have?

After studying history of art, Lisa started working in the nonprofit sector of the art world, initially running Milch, an independent arts space, before going on to edit artists' books at Book Works and lecturing in fine art at schools like Central Saint Martins.

Malin originally studied anthropology before embarking on an MA in creative curating at Goldsmiths. Ståhl initiated her own projects such as the artists' magazine *Happy Pappy*. Lisa and Malin also each have a master's degree in philosophy and contemporary critical theory.

— Where did you meet and when did you decide to open a gallery together?

We met when Lisa was the director of Milch, and Malin Ståhl was assisting there while completing her master's in creative curating. We decided to open a gallery in 2005, and Hollybush Gardens opened in September of that year.

— How did you choose the gallery name?

The name is taken from the street. We thought of various different names but decided to go for the street name to avoid symbolismn and metaphors and our own names.

— How do you choose the artists you work with?

We didn't open with a full list, but decided to progress as we went along. Some artists have been with us from the very beginning, and others have been added to the gallery at a later date. At times, artists are recommended to us by colleagues, other times an interest is awakened by an encounter with an artwork in an exhibition/studio/residency/project/art fair. Following an awakening of interest, we always make studio visits and talk to the artist in depth about his or her practice. Visually, the art that we represent can be quite diverse; there is not one recognizable style. We are interested in the aesthetics of the artwork, but it is equally important that the work/practice is rooted in a serious critical and conceptual engagement. We tend to be interested in art that arrives slowly and lasts for a long time.

— What is it in the work of an artist that makes you realize that it can go beyond the headlines and last in the long term?
How can anyone truly know? We see the gallery as a long-term project, and we like the idea of growing together with our artists, so we try and look at artists whose work doesn't only relate/respond to the latest trends. The qualities that often indicate that artists can stick around come from a commitment, but also crucially an openness that may allow for mistakes and experimentation. It is important for artists not to be too influenced and driven by trends in the market.

— Professionally, what's your greatest achievement?
It is probably an amalgam of things. We started the gallery with no money, and no experience of the commercial art world whatsoever, so we're happy with our progress to date. We are pleased with the collections we have placed work with, and that our artists are being invited to great shows. Achievement takes different emphases from one month to the next—perhaps it's a museum catalogue we've been very involved in, or finding colleagues whom you respect and can share with. In short, it is everything that contributes to our identity as a gallery.

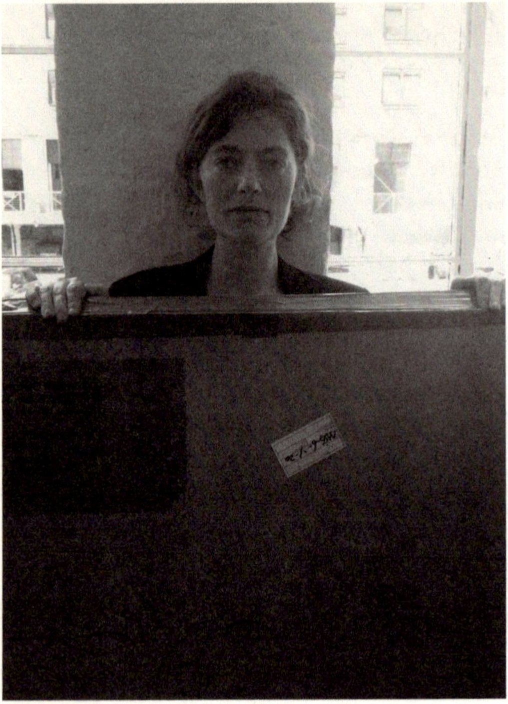

Lisa Panting

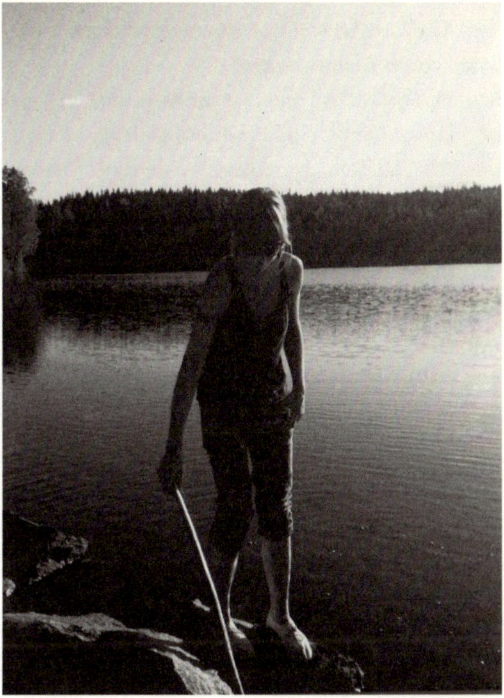

Malin Ståhl

— And, on the contrary, what is the mistake you wish you'd never made?
It's important to make mistakes—the art world is one of those curious places where mistakes can sometimes become valuable. For example, we didn't know who was who when we started out; however, these mistakes can also save you as you realize that most collectors forgive your initial naïveté and might like you in any case. Practically, we missed an artist we love by being a bit too slow.

— Is it difficult running a gallery in London? What are the city's greatest qualities and defects?
We lack any comparative experience, but we imagine it is relatively difficult in London. However, London craves the new, so it's open to new initiatives. If you are good and create a position, you will become visible, and you can find your way even if you have a small enterprise. The defects are obvious—space is expensive, it is competitive, and you need to work all the time.

— As a percentage, how many sales do you make each year in the gallery, and how many at fairs?
When we started, most of our sales were at the fairs, almost 80% during the first couple of years. But the balance starts to shift after you have been open a few years. We don't do that many art fairs, maximum three per year, and some are very good and others less so, so it's hard to give specific numbers.

— What do you think ought to disappear from the art world?

The idea that money is a passport to anything.

— What advice would you give someone who wants to open a gallery in London?

Don't think that there is a template: It is crucial to bring your own voice to the scene. Don't play it safe. But make sure this is really what you want to do and that you are doing it because you want to work for and with artists. It can be slow, painful, and costly, but you will develop amazing conversations over time. There are occasions when you see a new work by a gallery artist for the first time, and you get a feeling in your body . . . and you know that you've made the right decision.

Darren Flook

HOTEL, LONDON

— Hotel was originally located in your flat in Bethnal Green, where you invited artists to stay and showed their projects. It was a non-commercial space, so in order to make a living, you worked at Entwistle, while your partner, Christabel Stewart, worked at SHOWstudio. How did you choose artists at the time? Were you building a roster for your future gallery?

We shared a flat with artist Nils Norman, and when he decided to move out, we found ourselves with a spare room—3 meters by 4 meters—and an urge to do something that was ours. We had no money and this tiny space, so we thought, well, what can we offer? Why would anyone want to come here? The flat had always been a very social space, with artists and curators sitting around our dining table until the early hours, so it wasn't a huge leap to offer the spare bedroom out to people who were working on projects in London and needed a place to stay. At that time, a lot of small venues had the money for a budget airline ticket for an artist to come to London, but the hotels were prohibitively expensive. So that is how Hotel came about: One tiny room to show work, a spare room to sleep in, and a desire to do something. The first show was by Peter Saville, who had heard we were opening a space called Hotel and said he'd always wanted to make a "vacancies" sign. We said he could, and that was it. An empty space with a flashing white neon sign on the floor declaring VACANCIES. We like the idea of vacancies, possibilities, space, which coincided with the idea of a hotel, a space that is yours, for a time. The way we invited artists was very organic. We never researched in any formal way; art is part of our lives, and the artists were the people around us.

— What was your education? What brought you into the art world?

I did the usual art-school route: Foundation course followed by university. I started to curate shows of other students while still at university, and eventually found myself curating a public space in London, having stopped making my own work a few years before.

Christabel, Hotel's co-director, comes from an art-history and curatorial background. She lived and studied in Glasgow and then come to London to study at the Royal College of Art. She then worked on fig-1, curator Mark Francis's project that ran fifty shows in fifty weeks in a space in Soho. After that she developed concepts for SHOWstudio, a web-based art and fashion project. She continues to write and edit for magazines.

— I imagine Hotel started on a very small budget. Did this end up being an added value, in your opinion?
When we started, we worked out that we had £200 to do each show, not including production—four shows a year, £800. We immediately went over budget, and have been over budget ever since. I'm not sure if Hotel's lack of money was added value, but I think people liked the fact that someone was doing something that they could see themselves doing.

— You also had the good fortune to open your gallery just when the art market was at its most ebullient. The current financial crisis is creating serious problems, especially in England. What's your strategy today?
When we first opened we were nonprofit, as I was working for a commercial gallery and therefore couldn't do another commercial project on the side, and so the art market didn't really matter to us. Actually, we

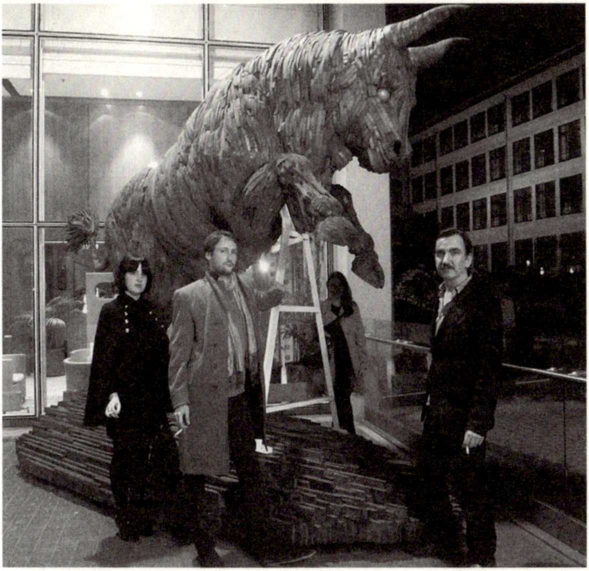

Hannah Robinson (Mary Mary), Tom Hanbury (Dicksmith Gallery), Christabel Stewart & Darren Flook (Hotel)

didn't sell a single thing until I left my job and we did the first Zoo Art Fair at the London Zoo, in October 2004. It was the fairs that really introduced us to the market, as our physical location—above a record shop on a backstreet in Bethnal Green—meant that we never met any clients in the gallery.
The crisis in England isn't as bad as the press likes to make out. The serious collectors are still engaged. The main problem with London is the cost of running a gallery, or any business for that matter. London is an expensive city, but the art market is global, and therefore London galleries have much higher costs while selling works at the same price as our friends in Los Angeles or Berlin. This has led to a few galleries having to reduce costs when the market slowed, but I haven't heard of a single serious gallery being in major trouble. The dinners are a little less flashy, but that is as much fashion as finance. Our strategy today is to concentrate on collectors we can work with closely—Italian, English, French, Belgian, Swiss and German clients; people, museums, and institutions we can visit and with whom we can collaborate without problems.

— In February 2009, you moved the gallery to a space in Whitechapel—now you have to leave home to go to work. How do you like the new premises?
First, in 2005 we moved from the apartment and took over the record shop below us, and that was great.

I loved, and still love that space, but the scale of work made by our artists changed, and we had to change with them. We were incredibly lucky to find this space in Whitechapel. After almost a year of searching, we were beginning to believe that the kind of space we had in mind just didn't exist any more, that every warehouse and factory in central London had been gutted and converted into live/work units and retail opportunities. But we found a street that wasn't already crowded with other galleries—we have always enjoyed standing a little to the left of everyone else—and yet is a five-minute walk from Whitechapel Art Gallery. The fact that the space wasn't going to kill us financially, had three-meter-high walls and skylights, and was six times the scale of our last space made it too good to turn down. And yes, after five years of working from home, it's nice to leave the house on a morning and walk to work. Like a real person.

— Who are your collectors? What percentage is English?

Our collectors are a very dedicated group. We never got picked up by the whole hedge-fund shopper crowd, I just don't think our aesthetic was shiny enough, and we have thus always worked with a small group of people who are incredibly serious about what they collect. As for nationality, we have a very wide range—if you want to work with serious collectors, you have to put in the effort to travel and search them out. The percentage that are English is I guess about twenty-five to thirty-five? I've never done the sums on that question.

— What advice would you give to a young person who wants to start collecting contemporary art?
Just spend a lot of time looking and thinking, and make contacts with young galleries as these will grow with you. There is great deal of great work out there, as well as an awful lot of trash, and price isn't any indicator of which is which. So pick an art fair or a magazine with a good reputation, and see whom they've selected. You'll hate most of it, but that's fine; it's just a way of giving you a little filter at the start. Also, enjoy it. You are not just buying a piece of work, you're taking part in an artist's life: You have just paid for a studio for a month, or for that new video camera. You are now part of the art world, and it's a fascinating place.

— Everyone has the idea that London is a very tough city. What do you think?
Every city has its issues—either it's too small, or too big, too expensive, or there's no collectors. I love London; it's exciting, both cutting-edge and ancient. It's also expensive and dirty and drives me insane. But London is about work and play, and as long as we want to do both of those, why would we live anywhere else?

— Some people say that the crisis will change the art world forever, and for the better, with only the best artists and galleries surviving. Do you agree with this?

This idea is actually quite funny. Why would only the best survive? Great collectors as well as tasteless people lost money in the crash, and there is no reason why a bad gallery shouldn't survive as long as there are enough tasteless people with money. And trust me, there are many tasteless people with money.

Georg Kargl

GALERIE GEORG KARGL, VIENNA

— Georg, unlike many young gallery owners, you didn't start by putting on exhibitions in your sitting room or in somebody's basement: In 1998, you opened a 350-square-meter space on three floors in Schleifmühlgasse, in Vienna. How did this happen? What is your background?

Actually, I did indeed start a sitting-room gallery, in the town of Krems-Stein in 1976—a little showing room in my mother's parents' house. After that, I started working in the antiques market, dealing in Art Nouveau objects and furniture, Vienna Modern, and Wiener Werkstätte. In 1989, I changed my focus to contemporary art, which was the real beginning of my current profession.

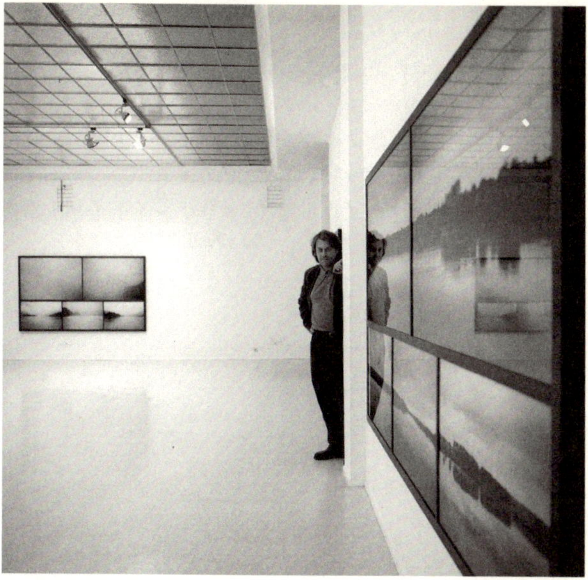

Georg Kargl

After running the gallery Metropol with a business partner in Vienna's first district until 1995, I was looking for an extraordinary space of my own, which I found at Schleifmühlgasse 5. As you said, it opened in 1998. One of the advantages of this exceptional space is that I can do both very small and really big shows. The 150-square-meter skylight hall of the former printing shop, for example, can be used to present large installations. I can also use the office and storage spaces.

— You were one of the first to open in the Freihausviertel area, which was pretty economically depressed at the time. With the opening of other galleries and a number of establishments and small boutiques, the district changed completely, and in just ten years, it has become a very chic neighborhood. What led you to choose this part of the city back then?

It was part of my plan to give this neighborhood a new look, integrating individuals in various fields in order to revitalize the surroundings for the community while also making it attractive to visitors. And, of course, I was lucky to find this special space.

— How did you choose the group of artists you work with?

I am looking for very individual personalities who have their own characteristic ways of thinking and working. I am always looking for "the true artist," as Bruce Nauman said: "The true artist helps the world by revealing mystic truths."

— How much of your gallery's sales comes from local collectors, and how much of your annual budget depends on sales at art fairs?

My main concern was, and still is, to deal with my community first and build up their interest in art. You always have to actively involve people to enrich their understanding of contemporary art, and they benefit from discussions about current artistic developments.

Half of the gallery's sales are to local and Austrian collections and half to international clients. I work on an international level and present the gallery's program at art fairs in Basel, Madrid, New York, London, Berlin, Turin, Düsseldorf, Zurich, and Ghent, in order to introduce the gallery to a wider audience.

— In addition to solo exhibitions of important artists such as Rudolf Stingel, Rosemarie Trockel, John Waters, Matt Mullican, Mark Dion, and Cerith Wyn Evans, your gallery presents theme-based group exhibitions. Here I'm thinking specifically of "Re-Production 2" from 2003 and "From Above" in 2004. Do you curate these shows yourself or do you turn to external curators?
It was "Re-Production 2," curated by gallery artist Thomas Locher, that showed me how theme-based group exhibitions could expand the reach of a gallery. Working on the exhibitions "From Above" and "*Zusammenhänge im Biotop Kunst*" (Relations in Biotop Art), which I curated in 2001 at Kunsthaus Mürz, Austria, I saw how much effort, time, and thinking they take. That's why I concentrate on group shows professionally curated by an art historian who works in the gallery. Fiona Liewehr has been developing theme-oriented shows for us since 2005. Her shows "Scene Missing" (2008) and "Feedbackstage" (2009) both traveled to Berlin, Galerie Thomas Schulte and "Feedbackstage" later went on to Kunsthaus Mürz, a museumlike kunsthalle in Austria.

— What was the best instinct you've ever had? And what, on the contrary, is the mistake you would never want to make?

I think the best and most lasting decision I made was taking the storefront of the Georg Kargl BOX. And producing *Oh Charley, Charley, Charley* and *Firetruck* by Charles Ray in 1992 and 1993, which introduced his work to the world, gaining a still-lasting appreciation. It is a mistake to believe this matters.

— Let's talk about the BOX. You opened this second exhibition space, which you use for special projects, in 2005. Could you briefly tell me how this project started?

The BOX was on my mind for many years, and it turned out that Richard Artschwager was willing to design the storefront for me. It took some more years for him to create the design, which was realized in collaboration with Artschwager and the architects Christian Jabornegg and András Pálffy. The architects were also responsible for the complete interior design of the BOX. This new space has made it possible to act flexibly and put on exciting projects by young or even well-established artists on a short-term basis.

— We are all influenced by important encounters. What were yours?

I had a very important moment when I visited an exhibition of works by Arnulf Rainer in 1971, when I was sixteen. It took my breath away. Another influential factor in my life was that I had to earn my living, which brought me to the antiques and design business at the age of twenty-one.

— Is there anything you detest or, at least, dislike about the work of a gallery owner?
Not everything that needs to be done in the business is convenient, but it has to be done.

— Can you give five good pieces of advice to a young person who would like to open a gallery in Vienna?
1. You have to build up your surroundings.
2. You have to trust in yourself in order to develop your own profile.
3. You should be a hub for your own generation, audience- and artist-wise.
4. You have to be careful in choosing your space and location. It should be in an existing, vivid, cultural surrounding or should have the potential for future urban development.
5. Be careful whose expertise you trust.

Karolina Dankow and Marina Leuenberger

KARMA INTERNATIONAL, ZURICH

— Your gallery name, Karma, is a fusion of your first names, an idea thought up by the artist Annelise Coste—nothing to do with Buddhism! How did the two of you meet and what, in fact, is your karma?
We met at university. We both studied art history in Zurich, and we went on university field trips together to Paris and Venice. That's where we first met, but we really got to know each other later, when Marina was working for Kunsthalle St. Gallen and Karolina was reviewing art shows as a freelance writer. Over dinner, we decided very spontaneously to do a show together. Karolina was living in a flat with a big, empty attic space, and we thought it would be a great place for a show. We invited Los Angeles-based artist Chris Lipomi, and we were thrilled that he agreed—after all, we were not much at that time! We did not have any experience, we had no money and not even a proper space. Still, we wanted to at least have a name. That's when Annelise came up with Karma International. She wrote us her idea by

text message, and we knew instantly that it was the right name for us. Kind of strange and with an esoteric twist, but the addition of "International" implies a professional and global side.
In the beginning, everything went very fast. Right after the first show, we immediately started planning the second one. It was a film screening we were able to do in cooperation with an institution in Zurich. Then a friend moved out of her painting studio and asked us if we wanted to rent it. It was very cheap and cozy, so we said yes. That's how we started the gallery. Without ever planning anything, Karma International just rolled . . .

— When you started in September 2006, your idea was to put on exhibitions of emerging international artists who had never previously shown their works in Switzerland. But you weren't exactly a gallery in those days. How would you describe it?
When we first rented the space, we were not a gallery in the sense that we did not represent any artists. Since everything went very fast we had no time to really think about our status. We were just working, doing shows, doing studio visits, inviting curators and artists. We also did fairs. Only three months after the very first Karma show, we went to a fair in Milwaukee organized by Scott and Tyson Reeder and John Riepenhoff.

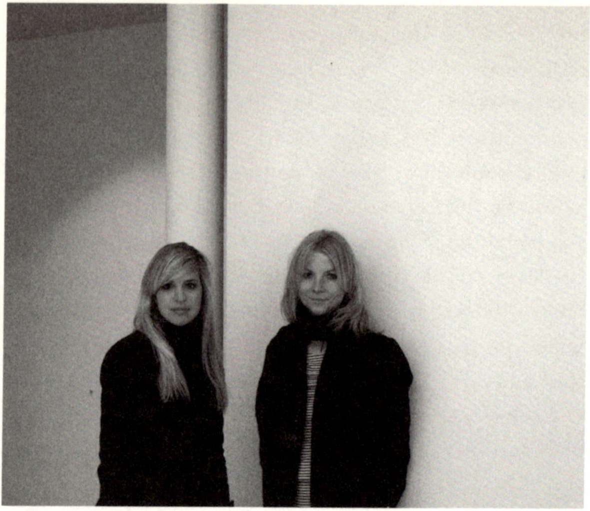

Karolina Dankow / Marina Leuenberger

Six months after the first show, we did the New Art Dealers Alliance fair in Miami. We were never against selling art, but it's true that Karma International started off more as a curatorial project than as a commercial gallery. We built up our artist program slowly, because we want to work only with people we are 100 percent sure about. Now we have six artists in our program. To be honest, we were never really interested in the question and status of being a gallery. We are convinced that strict classifications like off-space or commercial gallery are not appropriate to the twenty-first century. Nowadays, we need to rethink the concept of a gallery, and that's exactly what we are trying to do.

— What is your approach when you work with external curators? For example, Gianni Jetzer, director of the Swiss Institute in New York, has organized exhibitions in your gallery. Do you impose any conditions on the choice of artists? How does it work from a commercial point of view?

As we stated before, Karma International has always worked with a free spirit, and we like new and fresh ideas. That's why it's important to involve curators or artists who put together shows. When developing the concept of a show, we usually work very closely with the artists. We leave them full artistic freedom, but we support them with their choices and work. We have always worked on a low budget, so we do most transport ourselves, we build or paint walls, we get the material. Through this, we collaborate closely with artists and curators, and we are strongly involved in the whole process.

— I have read that you mostly show sculpture and installational works. Are you skeptical of painting?
Not skeptical, but we do think that it is not easy to find really good paintings.

— I agree. Yet you have found two painters.
Yes, we do have two wonderful painters in our program, Agnieszka Brzezanska and David Hominal. Both of them have great painting skills and a strong conceptual background. And they are not just painters, they are very good with other media, too.

— How do you choose your artists?
Mostly, we travel and meet new people. If we find somebody whose work we are fascinated by, we involve them in a show. If the collaboration is good—on a personal and artistic level—we might do a second, bigger project. By that time, we can decide if the person really fits into our program. And then we decide. It grows organically, and that's why it all fits together well.

— "Low-budget chic" has now become a guarantee of international success: If you want to capture instant attention in the art world, present exhibitions in your living room, and don't have work for sale—or at least, keep sales under the counter. Collectors and journalists will go wild. What's your view? And what makes your project so special?

We do not think too much about strategies. It's really good to have some money to realize projects, but people who start their businesses with too much money often lack creativity. We are still working ourselves up. We never pretended that we don't want to sell art. It is a wonderful business. As long as you don't sell out but really value art and never compromise. That might have been our only real strategy: We have always stayed true to what we are.

— Is there an aspect of being a gallery owner that you really can't stand?
Being a gallerist is certainly not an easy nine-to-five job, after which you go home and forget about your day over a gin tonic. We are thinking about art, the artists, and our business 24/7. But on the other hand, we chose this way of living, and we would never want to do anything else. Jokingly, we say if the gallery does not work out, we will open a bakery. But honestly, there is no plan B. We are committed. If we had to work for a big company or a boss, we wouldn't last a day.

— Seen from the outside, the art system in Zurich appears to be close-knit and collaborative, a community that values exchange and dialogue. Is that correct? And do public institutions play a part in this?
We have close collaborations with many institutions, such as the Migros Museum, where we had a film screening

with Agnieszka Brzezanska, and Kunsthalle Zurich, where we are part of PPT, a group that organizes events. We also have good relationships with many Zurich galleries. For the opening of the season at the end of August, we coordinated a weekend event called Rendez-View with several young galleries.

— What is the most interesting exhibition or project you've ever presented?
We can't say which show was the most interesting or the most important. With each experience, we have learned a lot about art, about curating, and about psychology; we grow with every single project. They all belong to Karma International history, and we wouldn't want to miss a single day of it.

— Your greatest intuition, and your worst mistake?
Honestly, many things we do come out of intuition. We trust our feelings, and so far this has worked out very well. So we have no intention on changing this; we will always trust our gut. If mistakes happen, we don't give them too much weight. It's normal that not everything will work out smoothly, and most problems come up for a reason. Sometimes you are angry or sad because you could not reach a certain goal, and afterward, a new opportunity comes up that is even better than what you were trying for in the first place.

Anton Kern

ANTON KERN GALLERY, NEW YORK

— When I was living in New York, between 2004 and 2007, I saw a series of wonderful exhibitions in your gallery. You have always had a top-quality program, possibly one of the most interesting in the whole city. After all, as the son of artist Georg Baselitz, you literally grew up in the art world, in constant contact with artists and dealers. What's the first thing you remember about this milieu from your childhood? When did you decide to devote yourself to art?

Well, it took me until quite late to really appreciate art. Yes, all sorts of people came to our house when I was a kid. But it was sort of a freak show, as I experienced it. Eccentric people. It was like living a gypsy or circus life. We moved a few times, the downside of which was that I changed schools and had to find new friends. It happened much later—I must have been eighteen already—that I really started to recount certain situations and prospered from it. My first piece of art was a silkscreen by Andy Warhol of Marilyn Monroe. It appeared on the invitation for Andy Warhol's show at Leo Castelli in 1966.

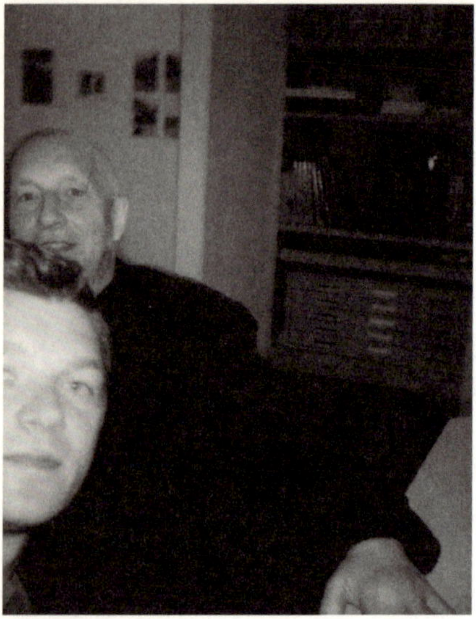

Anton Kern

— In 1996, at the age of thirty, you opened a gallery in Soho, in New York. Where had you worked before that? How did you train to run a gallery?
I worked at fairs at other galleries when I was a teenager, and later at an auction house. When I arrived in New York, I had an internship at the Museum of Modern Art. In fact, I stayed there for a year and a half. I also worked at Barbara Gladstone for a few years, until 1996, when she moved to Chelsea and I opened AKG at 558 Broadway.

— The list of your young artists is quite extraordinary—you've really been able to capture the spirit of the times. How do you choose your artists? Is there anyone else you trust to advise you?
It's really my personal choice. It's also important to me to meet the artist before working together. I do trust Nathalie Karg, my wife; she has a keen eye.

— Is there one exhibition to which you are particularly attached?
I seriously think that the first Manfred Pernice exhibition altered me.

— Which public exhibition space do you think is currently the most interesting in New York? And which private one?
I think New York has a number of great museums, obviously. It needs more ambition on a smaller scale.

— You tend to put on highly ambitious solo exhibitions. Do you interact with the artists or do you give them free rein?
It varies case by case; each show is different. I tend to bounce ideas around, and some of them stick.

— In your opinion, what distinguishes a good gallery director from a bad one?

I think it has seventy percent to do with taking full responsibility. The rest is intuition, love, and, of course, luck.

— Is there anything you can't stand about the art world? Anything you could do without?
Generally speaking, I like the whole thing. There are elements of it I can't stand, of course. But it's like any business, it's not fun and games.

— We all owe someone something. To whom do think you are most indebted? Someone to whom you owe your way of looking at and understanding art, for example.
Luck, that's whom I believe I owe a lot to.

— After spending a few years in Soho, you moved to much larger premises in Chelsea. Did your way of working change in the new gallery? How has the gallery program developed compared with the one in your first period?
I guess I matured a bit, as more people and artists were depending on me. I hope it's the same spirit, though.

— What's the greatest mistake you've ever made? And the best instinct you've ever had?
Not sure—I trust my instinct for the most part, and I'm looking forward.

Martin Klosterfelde

KLOSTERFELDE, BERLIN

— Let's start from the beginning. Who is Martin Klosterfelde? What is your background?

My parents are involved in the art world through publishing and collecting. I was raised with art, and after working at Barbara Gladstone Gallery in New York, and as an artist's assistant, I decided to open my gallery in 1995.

— You were one of the first gallery owners to open in the Mitte district in Berlin, in 1996. The art world has changed radically since then, and more visual artists live in Berlin than in any other European city. Do you think these changes have been entirely positive? Or is there something you miss about Berlin as it was then?

My first space was right in the center, on Linienstrasse, and it became too much. We are now moving to our third location. The increase in the number of resident visual artists, curators, and galleries changed the city completely. Visiting galleries has become much more of a mainstream activity; more people are interested, and there are different scenes.

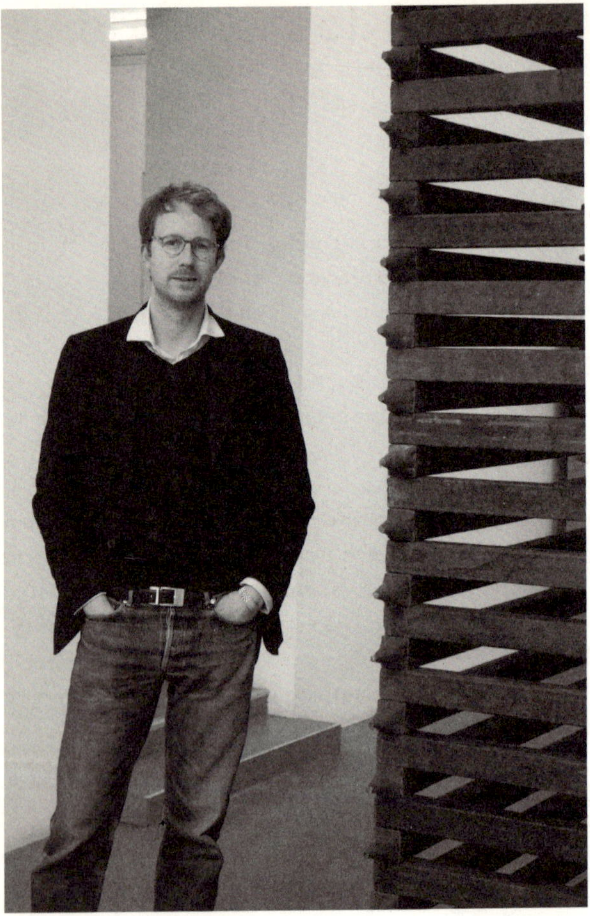

Martin Klosterfelde
Photo: Dominique Wenzel

— How did you choose your artists in the mid-1990s? I imagine you felt pretty free to work and experiment: Berlin was a city on the fringes and had practically no market. What was the art scene like?

I didn't really know what I was doing at the beginning. After I moved here from New York, I started working with artists from the US, such as Matthew Antezzo and Dan Peterman, and then later I started working with artists from the local scene. My first local artist was Nader Ahriman. Others, like Christian Jankowski and John Bock, followed shortly thereafter. The scene I was involved with, which interested me and was supportive, was that of Galerie Neu, Neugerriemschneider and all that went with it. Many nights were spent at Daniel Pflumm's bars/clubs, and all the artists from Berlin used to meet all the out-of-towners there. It was a very concentrated and constant dialogue. There were long nights with Franz Ackermann, Dan Peterman, and Rirkrit Tiravanija, and we would talk about all sorts of things. There was not really a market in Berlin in the mid '90s, and I never picked an artist for commercial reasons. The collectors who purchased came from out of town.

— You once said that private galleries put on exhibitions that are more interesting than those in institutional premises, such as museums. Do you think museums are a thing of the past? What should a contemporary art museum be today?

Museums are now more important then ever. Many muşeums, especially here in Berlin, missed the boat in terms of keeping up with their collections. Most of my artists are in international museum collections but not in the Berlin ones. Everything was really accessible and inexpensive at the beginning—all this has now changed. It's true that a lot of the galleries here started putting on exhibitions that were more on an institutional level and less commercial, as the pressure to sell was not as high here as in London and New York because the costs were lower. But the responsibilities of museums have not really changed.

— In 2001, you opened a new gallery in Zimmerstrasse, keeping the premises in Linienstrasse for site-specific projects. Was it a lack of space that made you move? How do you feel about the second gallery?
Yes, lack of space was my main motivation. I was also ready to move to a new location since that part of Berlin had become fairly mainstream. We have just moved again, away from Zimmerstrasse, because a huge building project made it impossible for the gallery to stay. We are now moving a little south of Potsdamerplatz and the Neue Nationalgalerie, a wonderful and still fairly undefined area considering that it is right in the heart of Berlin.

— How important are art fairs in the annual sales of your gallery?

Fairs are unfortunately very important for galleries like mine, because we make a lot of sales at them. It's about finding the right balance, since too many fairs can lower the quality of the work back at the gallery. During slower markets, I tend to do more fairs, because I have to.

— What is it that you're looking for in an artist? And what is it that you can't stand about collectors?

Great, unique, outstanding work with a long-term vision. A real collector is a real collector and I usually like these types. I really dislike people who call themselves collectors in order to buy art and then sell it at a profit.

— What would you have been if you hadn't become a gallery owner?

A gallery director.

— Have you ever thought of opening a gallery in another city? Would you ever leave Berlin?

Yes, I've thought about it many times, and I might one day open a second space somewhere, if it feels right.

Johann König

JOHANN KÖNIG, BERLIN

— You were born into the art world—your father is the renowned curator Kasper König—and you grew up among artists and artwork. When did you decide you were going to become a gallery owner?

First, I decided to work with artists. I wanted to be in direct touch with artistic developments and be involved in decision-making. I knew all kinds of careers in the art world, and what I always found most interesting and challenging was the power to make things happen. I realized that to become a curator or work in a museum organization would take quite some time and energy, and I wasn't really able to work in a regular office structure. I couldn't start as an intern, making photocopies, because my eyes weren't good enough because of an accident. So the answer to these problems was to open a gallery. I knew I would be able to work with artists and had a feeling for the right way of communicating their work. I wasn't so interested in the art market, but I quickly found out what's challenging about it.

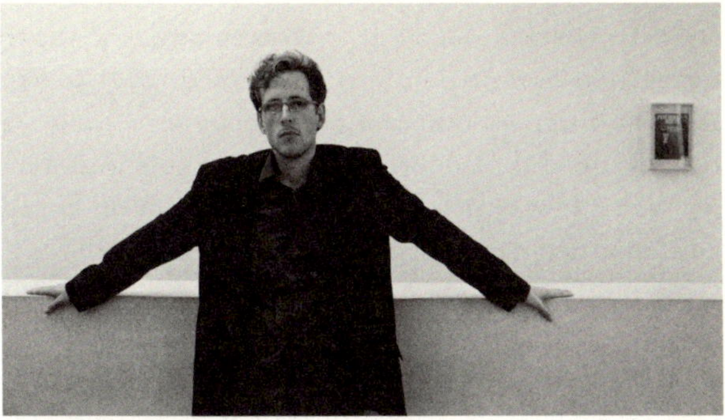

Johann König, 2008
Photo: Alexis Zavialoff

— What's your educational background? What did you study?

I studied economics in high school, as this allowed me to drop Latin in the tenth grade. I didn't go to college, which I regret now.

— In 2002, you opened your first gallery in Rosa-Luxemburg-Platz in Berlin, and in just seven years, you have become one of the most important and respected gallery owners in Germany. What's the secret behind this rapid success? How do you choose the artists you work with?

I think a key moment was Jeppe Hein's 2002 show, "360° Presence," in which a steel ball rolled around the gallery and slowly destroyed the space, until it was completely ruined. Prior to the show, everybody

tried to talk me out of it, as I was actually super broke and hadn't sold anything up to that point. Despite this, we had the piece produced, and we ruined the space. I somehow thought this would be my last show in any case, but we'd sold all three editioned events by the time of the opening.
From that point on, I just did what I thought would be right. Dialogue with my partner Kirsa Geiser was very important as well, as it's good to have another opinion and to have doubts; that's how your own opinion grows. As a gallerist, you are not only selling contemporary art, you are selling an opinion.

— What are the best and worst aspects of your personality?
I think I'm very open and have a natural interest in anything and everything. I can be very present and focused and can fully turn my attention to something or somebody. But I can be very absent as well.

— In recent years, German artists have had a massive presence on the market and in important international exhibitions. An Italian artist once offered to write an article for *Flash Art* called "Kraut Art." In your opinion, why has the German art scene gained such visibility? Is there such a thing as "German art"? And if there is, what are its characteristics?

I don't think there is such a thing as "German art"—maybe in painting schools, but that's not my field. I think Maurizio Cattelan was drawing a comparison with Italian art, which is of course not so present. I think this is definitely connected to the big institutional structures we have in Germany. But it's getting better in Italy—there's Micol Assaël!

— Right now, Berlin is undoubtedly the coolest city in Europe. Low rents have transformed Berlin into an ideal location for many generations of artists, making it a place to think, work, and concentrate. The only problem is its lack of a solid local market. Are things changing?

I think the market is pretty strong, as the level of interesting art is good at the moment. I've always thought the most important thing is to do good work, and I always focused on the program and on the artists. Collectors and buyers come automatically. And this is true in Berlin. Collectors are currently very involved, in production and trends; it's a very interconnected, interwoven scene.

— What proportion of your sales do you make at fairs, and how much do sell at the gallery?

I think it's about fifty-fifty. But fairs are not only points of sale; they are very important for collectors, curators, and maybe even for artists, because they can find galleries that share the same interests. Or, even more ideally, a fair helps shape interests. A good fair includes all sorts of galleries, all with a high level of quality—so you can find out which set of galleries you belong to.

— You often put on group exhibitions with a truly curatorial touch. Who organized the 2008 exhibitions "*Zuordnungsprobleme*" (Problems of Assignment) and "When a clock is seen from the side it no longer shows the time"?

Kirsa and I curated "When a clock . . ." together. It wasn't a big deal at first, but it turned out to be a great show. Originally, we had planned to do a show on performance leftovers—on how to deal with the remains of performances. Regarding "*Zuordnungsprobleme*," I always wanted to do a doubting but loving painting show.

— What is there other than art in the world of Johann König?

Hobbies you mean? Reading, swimming, and riding horses . . .

Tomio Koyama

TOMIO KOYAMA GALLERY, TOKYO

— My first question concerns the history of Japanese art. I am familiar with the Gutai group in the 1950s and the Superflat movement theorized by Takashi Murakami in the 1990s, but I don't know as much about the Japanese art scene in between. Tell me about the '70s and '80s.

I think that one of the artistic movements of the '70s that had has a strong influence on the history of contemporary Japanese art was Mono-ha. Lee Ufan and Kishio Suga, the most significant figures in this movement, are still active in the contemporary art scene. In the '80s, there were not many important movements, although some Japanese artists—such as Yasumasa Morimura, Tatsuo Miyajima, and Kei Funakoshi—started showing their work internationally.

— When you opened your gallery in the Sagacho neighborhood of Tokyo in 1996, Murakami was already known in Europe thanks to Emmanuel Perrotin. How did you get to know the artist? And how important was he for the development of your gallery?

I first met Murakami in 1990. I curated his first solo show at the Nippon International Contemporary Art Fair (NICAF), at the Shiraishi Contemporary Art (SCAI) booth.

Emmanuel's show at NICAF was with MA Gallery. I think he saw Murakami's works at that time. After that, I was the director of SCAI, where I organized two solo shows by Murakami, in 1994 and 1995.

When I opened my own gallery, Tomio Koyama Gallery, in 1996, I began representing Murakami. At that time, there was no market for his works. In 1997, I showed Murakami's *Miss KoKo* at the Liste art fair in Basel, but I wasn't able to sell it. I assume that Emmanuel was also having a hard time selling Murakami's "splash" paintings. I worked with Murakami until 2004, and he has his own gallery now. He gave me some wise advice for the management and organization of the gallery. But our perceptions of the arts—especially, how to produce artworks and sell them—were so totally different that we could not work together. Of course, I really respect him, but it's not my style.

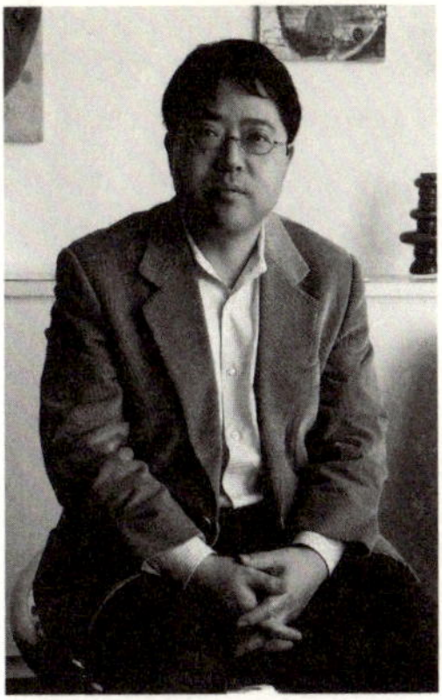

Tomio Koyama
Photo: Makiko Nawa

— In addition to Japanese artists such as Murakami, Yoshitomo Nara, and Masako Ando, you have worked with a number of Western artists, including Richard Tuttle, Tal R, Tom Sachs, and Franz Ackermann. Do they have a market in Japan?

Well, Tal R and Franz Ackermann have a market in Japan. The first show by Tom Sachs in Japan was very successful, but the second was not so good. This was because his works are too expensive for the Japanese art market, and I mainly sold Tom's works to clients in foreign countries. The works by Richard Tuttle and the philosophy behind them are very attractive to the Japanese, but there's no market for them, I'm afraid.

— How is contemporary art seen by most Japanese? The impression I get is that the language of contemporary Japanese artists such as Murakami, Nara, Masahiko Kuwahara, Tomoko Nagai, Mika Kato, Mika Ninagawa, and others is an organic part of popular visual culture. Is that really true?

Nara, Murakami, and Ninagawa have attracted so many people who are not art collectors. I think that's because they appear in many magazines. Nara's 2001 show at the Yokohama Museum of Art was attended by more than 90,000 people, and Ninagawa's show at the Tokyo Opera City Art Museum had 60,000 visitors. In Japan, artists such as Nara, Murakami, Ninagawa, and Yayoi Kusama have been shown in the popular fashion museums and attract young girls, too. However, many artists are not that well known in general, although they are known by art lovers.

— Japan is going through an acute financial crisis this year, even tougher than the one hitting the European economy. How are things going for your gallery? How are your sales at art fairs?

Frieze and Art Basel Miami in 2008 were very bad. We sold seventy percent less than the previous year, and we had deficits at both fairs. On the other hand, at Art Basel in 2009, we sold quite well. Although thirty percent down from the previous year, we nevertheless made a profit.

— Are there any differences between Japanese and Western collectors, in their way of collecting and looking at art?

Japanese collectors find a spiritual aesthetic in collecting fine art, so they don't go to the secondary market to resell what they have. Whereas in Western society, people frequently sell works at auction. This means that Western collectors are good at confirming their collections through auctions. In Japan, more and more information about the art market is circulating, but market is not well formed.

— What would you have done if you hadn't become a gallery owner? Is there another great passion in the life of Tomio Koyama?

I wanted to be a movie producer.

Jose Kuri and Monica Manzutto

KURIMANZUTTO, MEXICO CITY

— The two of you set up your gallery in 1999, with Gabriel Orozco and thirteen other artists. Initially, Kurimanzutto didn't even have an exhibition space, creating events and situations in different sites and contexts. If I'm not mistaken, the first was called "*Economia de Mercado*," and it lasted one day: You showed works of art in a normal fruit and vegetable market, and the artworks had the same prices as the vegetables. Then you showed films in theaters, put on shows in commercial stores, and then went to Paris, where you turned Chantal Crousel's gallery into a sort of squat. Those who saw the exhibition remember the absolute chaos and cheerful mood. What was the basic reason for these initial activities of yours?

Probably the main reason why the gallery was born was because there was the need for it. Not because there were good art schools, or because there were interesting museums or institutions, and not because of the thriving market, or because of the existence of an art system, but because the most important thing was there: a really good group of artists. It was not difficult to see that something very important was going on—you could feel the electricity in the air. At the beginning, most of our effort consisted of giving shape and direction to what was already happening. Our activities responded to the way artists related to their ideas and the context.

— About a year ago, in October 2008, you opened your new gallery in Mexico City: a vast inside-out space that even has a Japanese-style garden. The opening was quite an event, reported even in the US. In just ten years you went from being an "unofficial" gallery to part of the international art establishment. How has this affected you? Could you give us an overview of this decade?

Basically, we are still working in the same way, very close to the artists in a sort of complicity—this has remained unchanged. The relationships are actually deeper now, as we share many more things than we did ten years ago. We also like change: contexts change, conditions change, politics change, people change.

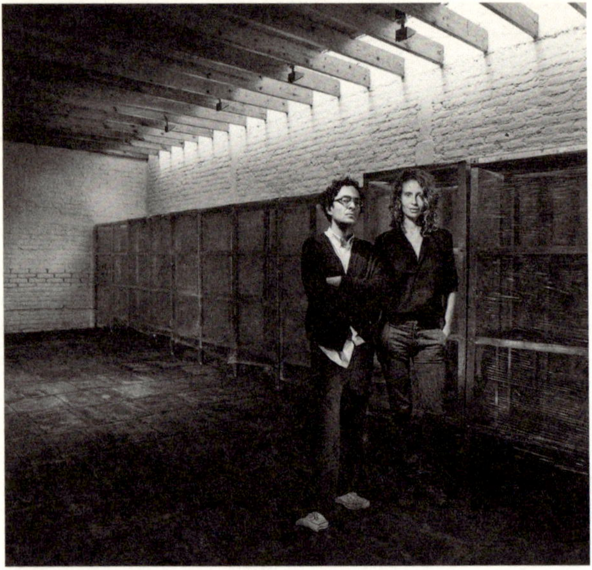

Jose Kuri/Monica Manzutto
Courtesy of kurimanzutto, Mexico City
Photo: Fernando Montiel

We are always challenged by how the world is changing, and we try to understand it and make the best of it. We also take full responsibility for growing up, as we cannot remain at the same stage all our life. Experience is something we value. We have many more opportunities now, different ways to develop. Although we think quite locally, our actions now have more international resonance.

— The first exhibition in your new premises had to do with the idea of bookcases in artists' studios. How do the ideas for your exhibitions come about? Do you discuss ideas and projects with your artists?
We maintain constant dialogue with the gallery's artists. Some ideas for shows come directly from them, some are put on the table by one of us and take shape in discussion. Every artist has his or her own individuality, and we are not curators, but as a gallery we are very good at working as a team. It does not mean that everyone contributes in the same way, is equally involved, or even agrees on everything, but we do see the gallery as an artist's gallery. Even the direction we take is shaped by the artists—their opinion is what we value the most, and sometimes it's the hardest critique as well.

— The phenomenon of collecting in Mexico is different from that of other Latin American countries, and it has an interesting tradition. Some important collectors are intellectuals, such as Carlo Ashida, or the philosopher and curator Patrick Charpenel, who started collecting art at the age of eighteen, in the 1980s. In the past twenty years or so, a new group of young, very rich, and determined entrepreneurs has begun collecting, people like Eugenio López Alonso, Cesar Cervantes, Agustin Coppel, and Aurelio López Rocha. What is your general opinion about the art system in your country? What do you think is missing in Mexico?

When we started the gallery there were three or four really good collectors, very well informed, taking risks, and collecting in a challenging way. We feel proud that they were very supportive of our initiative. Eugenio López and Patrick Charpenel were of fundamental importance, but we did ninety-five percent of our sales abroad. That's not true any more. Slowly and with a lot of work things have changed, and there are now many more people interested in and committed to contemporary art. The best collections are never those of the very rich. We try to work with collectors who have their own, personal voice. Collections that can portray a complex view of the moment we live in.
We are happy to see more galleries opening, and the system is becoming more professional. But we need museum and institutional collections to become far more active, to show Mexican art in all its diversity and history—not only the contemporary but also the fantastic modernity that Mexico experienced in the late 1940s and '50s. We would love to see a very strong museum of modern art. We need people researching and writing art history, understanding the past and comprehending the present. A country with no memory is a country with no future.

— How are you coping with the international crisis? Do you think it might also have a positive effect on the art system?

First of all, Mexico has been in crisis for as long as we can remember, so it comes as nothing new. It does not have to determine the way you think and act. If it takes up too much of your time, then you are using your energy in the wrong way; it is just one factor in a long equation. In another sense, we believe it's a moment of great opportunity, and it's helping to put things in perspective.

— The curators of the 1989 Whitney Biennial—Richard Armstrong, Richard Marshall, and Lisa Phillips—wrote in the catalogue for that year that "capitalism has overtaken contemporary art, quantifying and reducing it to the status of a commodity." This comment seems as relevant as ever. In the past few years, works of art have been transformed into objects of pure speculation—we've seen dealers buy works and put them back on the market six months later.

This is a sign of the times we're living in; it is just the consequence of greater economic and ideological order. Nothing to be surprised about. Money has too much value as compared to many other things, like ideas, ethics, sense of humor, etc.

— What advice would you give to a young collector today?

Honesty, be yourself.

— The happiest moment and the most dramatic moment in your career?

The happiest is always working on new ideas.
The most dramatic is always flying coach on a full transcontinental flight.

— Let's end with your beginnings. What was your academic background? What made you enter the world of art?

Monica studied international affairs in Mexico and worked at Marian Goodman Gallery in New York. Jose studied economics in Mexico and got a master's degree in public policy in New York. Art has always been the most useful tool to understand what we are and where we live. We are entirely devoted to it.

Michèle Maccarone

MACCARONE INC., NEW YORK

I am so sorry, I wrote my responses to the interview on my computer, and it was pretty focused. But then, typical me, I didn't save it, and it was deleted, so now I have redone it on my BlackBerry on a bus on my way out of town, so it might be a little difficult to follow. I answered several questions at once, and I apologize if this is going to make more work for you.

I left Luhring Augustine in 2000 quite exasperated! After quitting my job as director, I spent months considering my next step—what it was I wanted to do, and if I was indeed going to remain in the milieu that I had just left. There was a running joke that I should curate the Carnegie International—and you know, that still does not sound like a bad idea.
In this hiatus period of about one year, I curated shows, traveled, and made many studio visits. Over the years, I had amassed a network of artists I was in dialogue with. Ultimately, it wasn't my intention to open a gallery. I never had an interest or inclination

to sell art or even run a business. But at the same time, my independent nature made me pretty much unemployable. So 45 Canal Street happened quite accidentally. I stumbled upon this decrepit nineteenth-century building on the edge of Manhattan. The awning bore the name KUNST, and this was a sign (literally) for me that I needed, wanted this building. It inspired me to act; it activated a sense of urgency and encouraged me to want to put on exhibitions and commission projects. I just needed a space to do this in, and here it was. I never thought about the financial ramifications of opening a small business, I didn't have a business plan. I had this idea of inviting artists to make exhibitions, and I just went for it. And the building inspired some amazing shows. The physical context was unlike any traditional exhibition space, and artists really reacted to it.

Regarding freedom—or the idea that I was free to do as I wished—yes, I collaborated with the artists I wanted to work with. But at the same time, we are never that free—in my case, I was constantly fighting poverty and a disorganized approach to the business end of things. But 45 Canal Street was the departure point for the works that were created there. Most notably Christoph Büchel's inaugural exhibition, which interacted with the building by destroying and building the space all at once. It set a precedent for the

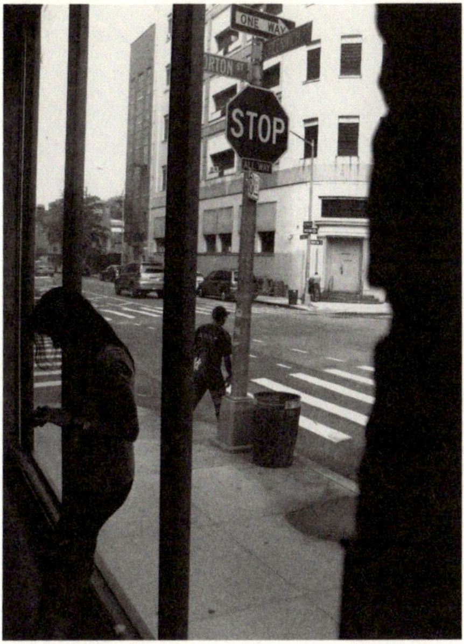

Michèle Maccarone

ambitious and radical type of installations that were mounted in that space. It was a hard show to follow, but Christian Jankowski, who did the second one, made a video, *Point of Sale*, which directly related to the way I inhabited a space that was occupied by an electronics store (Kunst). The video made comparisons between the two small businesses that were operating simultaneously in the same building.

In the nascent stages of developing the gallery program, all the artists were chosen very carefully and all met certain criteria I was particularly interested in. At that time, I wanted to collaborate with artists who worked on a project-to-project basis, and the results would be manifested in a variety of media. I wasn't so interested in artists who had a certain style and strict studio practice, but in those who were investigating themes on a broader level—and I think that is why I was showing so many site-specific installations and videos. Now, things have changed quite drastically. I am more interested in anchoring historical artists in the program. I am working less with installations, and the artists are less of a tightly curated group. (When I first opened the gallery, a curator said that my program was like a tightly curated group show—I never knew if this was a compliment or not.) I am still showing artists I want to show, and the program keeps morphing. I like this moment. I am experimenting and doing more one-off projects with artists.

I am maturing—when I opened the gallery I was twenty-six, now I am thirty-five. At a certain point, I had to get the hell out of Canal Street—after five years it was played out. The roof was about to collapse, we had no heat, and my staff all threatened to quit. Chelsea wasn't for me. I have never been able to do what I am supposed to, make solid business decisions and keep to the status quo. In spite of myself, I have always gone against the grain.

The thing I hate most about being a gallerist is MONEY and having to deal with business. I wish I could just sit and think—I feel like I never have enough time. I spend all my energies trying to keep the gallery afloat and my doors open.

As regards collectors, I hate it when they place works on reserve and keep them there, collectors who never pay, and canceled sales.

The trouble with the art world is precisely that it is an "art world," for it has overwhelmed the real work: art. Art fairs should be eradicated. I probably shouldn't say this, but they take away from the real work we should be focused on, which is exhibitions, artists. I am so happy now that I am not doing any more fairs. They were a distraction and took an emotional toll on me.

My biggest mistakes were never being financed properly, spending money on production—money that I did not have—and putting the gallery in debt. I did so many uncommercial, unsellable shows because I believed in the projects, not thinking about the financial impact. But I am proud of the shows that I did and the rigor and intensity that critically established the gallery. All I was thinking about was the integrity of the artists and their exhibitions. But maybe the financial risk I took wasn't such a mistake in the end—it just meant that I had to struggle. And struggling somehow seems authentic to me.

And I love the last question.[1] In the end, a gallery is a shop—sometimes things fly off the shelves, and sometimes things end up in storage. Every show is different, and in the end, it is business as usual. I am there to show and (on occasion) sell art. I don't see myself as a revolutionary at all. Some people have this misconception that I am crazy. I just think I'm human.

[1] The *New York Times* published an article by Roberta Smith on January 13, 2006, in which she wrote about you, "Her current exhibition, the overstocked debut of Nate Lowman, demonstrates the way all galleries fluctuate between subversion and business as usual, if only to survive." What's your opinion of that statement? Do you feel a bit like a Capuchin-style revolutionary, to use an expression from Céline?

Hannah Robinson

MARY MARY, GLASGOW

— You started out as an artist. When did you decide to change tack, and how did you decide to open an exhibition space?

At art school, I always felt much more comfortable discussing, discovering, and thinking about other people's work than making my own. I was never very good at it anyway, and I had been organizing and putting on shows in flats and found spaces during college, so it felt like a natural progression to open a project space in my flat after I left. It was a way to show and get to know better the work I liked by people I knew from Glasgow and art school. At that time, many of the artists I showed weren't doing or hadn't done shows elsewhere, so essentially and quite simply it was a way to offer them the opportunity to show and make new work, and to give me the chance to get to know them and their practices better.

The decision to open as a commercial space happened quite organically, mainly from wanting to bring a wider audience to the work I was showing and continuing a longer-term and more in-depth relationship with some of the artists that I had got to know through the flat exhibitions, which always felt too transient for me. In addition, some of the artists had mentioned that they would like to work with me if I opened a space. I remember we did a show with Karla Black quite early on. To aid in writing the text for the show, she sent us a list of works and some images of artworks that had a huge influence on her and her work, and this was really important for me. It felt like such a privilege to be let into someone's practice like that, for them to open up what is quite a personal and private thing. Representing artists seemed the best way to continue this and have this kind of relationship and experience all the time.

— Mary Mary started out as an artist-run project. What sort of artists did you show in the early days?
We showed many of the artists I work with now, such as Karla Black, Nick Evans, Sara Barker, Aleana Egan, Lotte Gertz, Lili Reynaud-Dewar, along with a few artists from London and Germany—all of whom had pretty much just graduated. We also held screenings and quite a few artists' talks.

— In 2006, Mary Mary opened as a commercial gallery. How did you choose the artists you would work with, and why are they almost all women?
As I say, it happened quite organically. The majority that we began representing had done shows with me in the project space, and/or I had been to art school with them, so I had gotten to know their work over a

period of time already; others then got added to the list over the next couple of years. There is no grand scheme as to why I work with these particular artists, it's simply the work that I'm drawn to and have a connection with. This is the same as to why there are more women than men. There is no plan for this, and I don't make a distinction, as this ends up being very restrictive. I feel quite uncomfortable about work being defined as being made by women or as "women's art."

— Where does the name Mary Mary come from?
It's from Mary Shelley and her mother, Mary Wollstonecraft.

— Over the past ten years or so, Glasgow has become one of the most significant centers of art in Europe. What do you think makes the city's art scene so interesting?
There are many more artists here than galleries, and so there is a really strong peer group for artists to work with and play off of. In comparison to other art centers, artists here are able to just get on with their work pretty much unhindered, which makes for strong, mature practices. The weather is quite bad, too, so people end up staying in their studios much more than they probably would if we were basking in the sun all the time! The art

school also forms a really strong foundation, and places like Transmission Gallery offer a strong sense of community and opportunity early on in artists' careers, which is so important.

— Is there anything you can't stand about running a gallery? And what is it that gives you the greatest satisfaction?
Well, the gallery is only three and a half years old, which means that so far there isn't anything I would say I can't stand, but there are, of course, some things I like doing better than others—I'm not a huge fan of practical, technical installation stuff. The greatest satisfaction is probably seeing artists on their way to getting to where they deserve to be, and to where you always thought they would get from the beginning. Introducing work to new people and seeing them build a relationship and understanding of the work is also great.

— In your opinion, what makes a good gallery director? What qualities do you think the ideal gallery director should have?
Enthusiasm, patience, energy . . .

— The art market is going through a very tough crisis at the moment. What's your survival strategy? At the moment, how much of your turnover comes from sales at art fairs, and how much from the gallery itself?

I'm just keeping going with the gallery's program and fairs and being a bit more careful with what we spend money on and when we spend it. I think it's really important to try to carry on with an ambitious and dynamic program and not let this be affected. I'm keeping an eye on things much more and making sure we aren't wasting money or spending money when and where we don't need to. I think I'm double-checking much more before I make decisions.

As Glasgow doesn't have a collector base, the majority of the gallery's turnover has always come from fairs or as a direct result of them.

— How do you see your future and that of Mary Mary? Describe a best-case scenario.

The best-case scenario would be to continue working with the artists I do now alongside a broader, more international program, and for the artists to all be doing well, in terms of institutional shows and so on. I would also like to see the publishing side of the gallery develop more.

— What is the purpose of art?

I haven't got a definitive answer for this one I'm afraid, and I'm not sure it's something I can put in a little sound bite!

Massimo Minini

GALLERIA MASSIMO MININI, BRESCIA

— You and I have a lot in common: a love of contemporary art, a passion for prehistoric archaeology. You worked for Giancarlo Politi's *Flash Art* in Milan in the early 1970s, and I worked for the magazine in New York from 2004 to 2007. What's your educational background? Who is Massimo Minini?
Massimo Minini is a lawyer manqué, like Ugo Mulas, and an archaeologist manqué. Afraid of blood, so medicine was out, too. A dunce in mathematics, so engineering was a no-no. And that's how I found myself running a gallery. Classical studies in high school, law at the Università Statale in Milan from 1964 to '68, and then a rollercoaster of jobs. I worked rather unenthusiastically in Brescia, then a love affair went sour, and I was back in Milan. That rogue Politi enchanted me with his witchery (with gallery owner Pio Monti as his accomplice), and I fell into the trap of art. I had become involved with art in Milan, when I should have been in the halls of the Statale.

As for my interest in prehistory, that comes from my background. I was born in Vallecamonica and was fascinated by the discoveries that were made all around me. I went on two summer digs with Emmanuel Anati, the great archaeologist and pupil of Abbé Breuil, and I'm still close to that world today.
There's no contradiction between pluperfect and present: I find an enormous sense of continuity.

— You once told me an interesting anecdote about how the *Art Diary*—the directory of galleries and museums, artists, and arts professionals—really started up. It was something to do with Willoughby Sharp, who founded *Avalanche* magazine. Could you tell it again?
Willoughby came and met us in Milan. The magazine had made him a legend. He sat down in the studio and started phoning left, right, and center, as everyone did in those days, leaving us with the bill to pay. Giancarlo was a bit annoyed, but then came his Gyro Gearloose–style light-bulb moment. He saw Willoughby's neatly written address book, packed with names. Wow! What an idea! And that was how *Art Diary* was born.

— What was *Flash Art* like in those days? And why did you decide to leave and open a gallery?
Flash Art was great: tabloid-style and black-and-white. I had a subscription before I worked there.

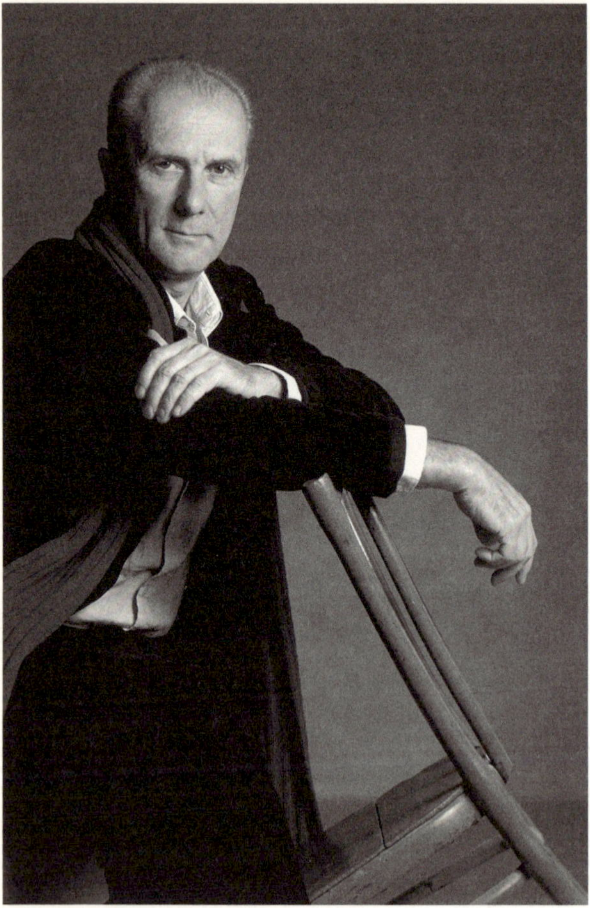

Massimo Minini

We used to wait for it anxiously to find out what was going on in the world. I was hired in November 1971 and got to see it from the inside. I was in charge of organization (it really was disorganized), and I oversaw subscriptions, advertising, distribution, and contacts. I already spoke a couple foreign languages well, and I was the promotion manager. We did Gino De Dominicis's Biennale and Harald Szeemann's Documenta like a dream. I used to sell the works that galleries gave us instead of paying for advertisements. And so I learned to sell. Toward the end, I was doing a bit of insider trading. If I saw a lovely work, I might buy it myself (and then sell it). Something one shouldn't do. So Politi and his new partner, Gino di Maggio, took my scalp, and in 1973, after Pinochet's coup, I found myself out on the street. So what could I do? Without a lira in my pocket, I returned to Brescia, reestablished my old contacts, worked enough to eat, and opened a gallery in the afternoon with Enrico Pedrotti. He had the space, and I had the know-how that I had picked up in my two years at *Flash*, and I'm grateful to Giancarlo for this. Who knows what I would have done if it hadn't been for him. I might be selling bars of soap.

— Why did you decide to open a gallery in Brescia? With all its artists and collectors, Milan would have been a more natural choice—not to mention Turin and Rome.

I couldn't have afforded the rent in Milan. In Brescia, it was free. The gallery Zero opened in Piacenza some years later. In Brescia, I had a family, my own home, and my little girls at school, as well as the gallery. I must admit, I was also a bit lazy when it came to changing my life, friends, and affections. And then came fax machines and computers and art fairs, and it wasn't so essential to be in a big city anymore. Also, in Brescia I was free to show artists I could never have had in Milan because of the competition. Actually, I found myself in a strange situation, although it seemed quite normal back then. Even those who were in towns on the outskirts had access to great artists. Markets were local in those days. But I realized, just a moment ahead of my competitors, that things were about to go global. So I was able to represent the giants of my day, which would be impossible now because of the excessive power of a system that has taken over the market—what I refer to as the "supermarket."

— Which artists did you first work with, and how did you choose them?

I met Daniel Buren, Joseph Beuys, Victor Burgin, Giorgio Griffa, Giulio Paolini, Marcel Broodthaers, and Sol LeWitt at the legendary Documenta and Biennale in '72. I understood their importance, and I asked them to work with me. Some of them accepted. Initially, the "greats" were slightly suspicious—they didn't know what I would do. And even I didn't know myself. Buren, for example, told me, "Get on with your gallery and your exhibitions, and send me the invitations. In three years' time I'll say yes or no." I should add, though, that after a year and three months, his answer was "yes."

— Whenever I see you, you're always enthusiastic, cheerful, tireless, and about to get on a plane (or just getting off one). It seems you have an unconditional love of what you do. Is there anything you don't like about the job of running a gallery? Something you would happily do without?
I would happily do without selling. That's the part I like least. You often have to apply pressure and convince hesitant people to buy. Sure, it's also interesting—it's a testing point, where your skill shows through. Pushing your opponent over the precipice of perdition. Even so, I would be happy to run a museum. Basically, the best museum curators are former gallery directors. Just look at Ida Giannelli.

— Many people believe that the crisis is good for art, and that only the best will survive. What do you think?
I think the sharks are more likely to survive than the cherubs. One can't predict that only the best will

survive, in part because I think that this time something really is going to change. After this is over, the world won't be the same again. If it is, then we're a bunch of idiots who don't give a shit about anything and only try to grab what we can.
What I mean is that the system is in crisis. We—possibly just a few of us—are aware that the world is full of stuff and that we can't just focus on quantity, as in the past, without courting disaster. We ought to focus on quality instead. We went and made the same mistakes as in 1990, and even worse because the system was even more bloated, richer, and better equipped. They used to say, "Things are different now, there's a broader base." Absolutely true. So there's further to fall.
Unfortunately, I'm a convinced millenarian, and I know the apocalypse is coming. Possibly just a few years later than prophesied. Man stops at nothing, except his own death. This time death might come not to the individual but to the world, or at least to an open-ended system of development. We'll see. I think that if we don't go back to reasonable quantities of everything, will meet the destiny of rats.

— Is there an artist, or any other person, who changed your way of looking at art?
Salvo and Paolini. The devil and holy water. Paolini once said he liked Salvo because Salvo was the only

one in Turin who didn't copy him. It was Paolini who taught me beauty, as well as understatement—which, alas, I didn't learn that well. Salvo got me fascinated in the idea of the self-made man, the self-taught, cultured person, the artist who returns to order after disorder.

They say that Leonardo Sciascia, writer and politician, wanted "*Contraddisse e si contraddisse*" ("He contradicted others and he contradicted himself") as the epitaph on his tombstone. Supposedly, it wasn't allowed. I'll go to Racalmuto, where he's buried, and check. If it's not there, I'll see if I can get it on mine.

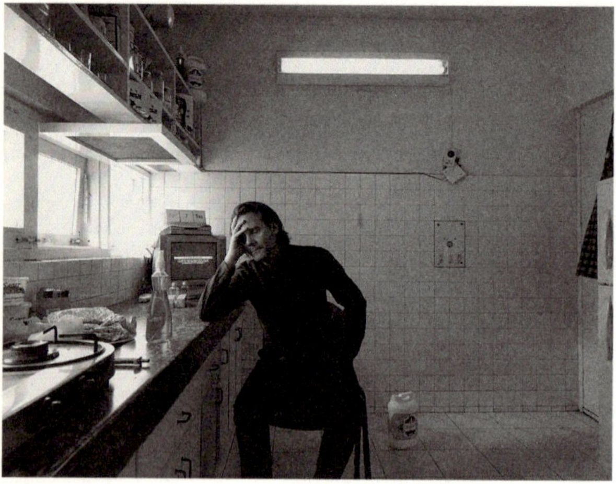

Peter Nagy
Photo: Bharat Sikka

Peter Nagy

NATURE MORTE, NEW DELHI

— The crisis in the late 1980s radically changed the New York art system. You had a gallery in the East Village, also called Nature Morte, which closed more or less when the market was slowing down. And, of course, everyone met the same fate, with the exception of just four or five galleries that managed to survive, and moved to Chelsea. As a veteran, then, what's your opinion about this latest crisis? What has changed in the art world, and what will always remain the same?

I closed Nature Morte in New York in the summer of 1988, while the market was still strong. I closed it because the East Village was coming to an end as a neighborhood for galleries, and to keep it going I would have had to move it to Soho (as many East Village galleries did do, as you know). But I was successful as a painter at the time, so I had no desire to continue with the gallery in New York. But, in the back of my mind, I did know that I would open a gallery again some day, somewhere else—basically, because I do not like teaching and would prefer to run a gallery and be involved in the market.

That said, the art market crash in the fall of 1990 did affect my decision to move to India. My first trip was in April/May 1990. It was a standard three-week trip to northern India (New Delhi, Agra, Jaipur, Udaipur, and Bombay). After that, I planned to go for a stay of one year, from November 1992 to September 1993. I wasn't really thinking about what would happen after that, but I stayed on, and by 1994 I had started considering opening a gallery there. Nature Morte opened in New Delhi in November 1997.

To answer your question about the current "crisis." Of course, the art market is always connected to larger financial systems. And we have just lived through an insanely robust art market over the past five or six years. I think, in some ways, the current situation is a necessary cleansing period, when the market can adjust itself, but also a testing time for artists and galleries, to see who is in it for the art and not just the quick and easy money. In this way, the art world has not changed. But the art business has changed profoundly, due to the internet and e-mail, so our clients are much more diverse, and many never actually come to the gallery in New Delhi.

— You moved to New Delhi before the Internet age, however. I imagine you must have felt very cut off there. What made you decide to live there?

Yes, I caught the tail end of an India that was profoundly disconnected from the rest of the world. I went because I was infatuated with India and its culture on many different levels, so I wanted to live there and learn more about it.

— As you said, you opened a gallery again only in 1997. What did you do in the meantime?
I learned about India! I read a lot and traveled around the country. I had very little money, so I had to go slowly. But I was also working on putting the pieces of the gallery together: finding funding, finding Indian partners (as a foreigner, I cannot open a business in India without Indian partners), meeting artists, etc.

— Why did you use the same name, Nature Morte? Was there perhaps something in the Indian art scene that reminded you of the East Village in the 1980s?
I kept the name Nature Morte because it was a brand name known in the United States and Europe, and people knew it was my gallery. It wasn't known in India, and it did work against me there as people thought it was a weird name and didn't know what it meant. But one of the reasons I stayed in India and wanted to open a gallery there is because I discovered a generation of artists who were working with many of the same ideas and issues that I had been involved

with in the '80s in New York—appropriation, theories of gender and identity, how the influence of mass media was affecting art practice, political and theoretical frameworks for art—albeit applied to their own context. This mixture of the familiar with the new was very exciting for me.

— Do you think there's a positive side to the crisis?
It's always healthy to find the positive aspects of bad situations. The crisis has already made the speculators—the "flippers"—disappear, and many people who opened galleries just to manipulate the boom market are closing up. As I said, it seems like a natural ebbing and flowing of the art system in general.

— What will you do next?
I have no intention of closing the gallery in New Delhi for at least another ten years. In partnership with New York's Bose Pacia, we opened a space in Calcutta, Bose Pacia Kolkata, in March 2007. Then in November 2008, we opened a space in Berlin, called Nature Morte Berlin, which will be more difficult to keep going. It will depend on the broader financial scenario.

— What about your activity as an artist?
I never stopped being an artist, although I have had almost no time to produce art in the past few years.

But I have also been busy as a writer on art while in India, and that has not slowed down. I had a solo show of my paintings with the Chemould Gallery in Bombay in 2004, and the slowdown in the market may mean that I have more time to spend on making art again.

— Could you give some advice to someone wanting to start a collection of Indian art?

Do your homework and a lot of research. Luckily, information about Indian art is quite accessible as the art world of India is conducted almost entirely in English.

— What does India mean to you today? Would you ever leave?

I define myself as a "New Yorker who lives in India." I'll stay here for the rest of this life, although hopefully not chained to New Delhi. Of course, I travel a lot, and this will probably continue for the next few years, at least. But if you like India, most of the rest of the world can seem like a rather dull place.

Tim Neuger and Burkhard Riemschneider

NEUGERRIEMSCHNEIDER, BERLIN

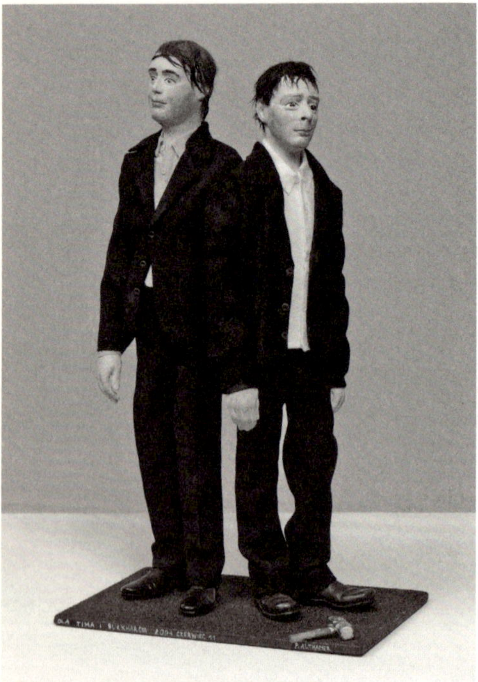

Pawel Althamer
Dla Tima I Burkharda, 2004

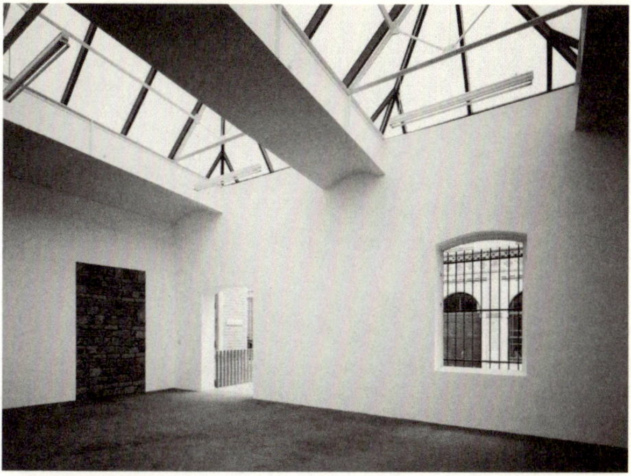

Rirkrit Tiravanija
Untitled, 2001 (no fire no ashes)
1.06.2001 – 24.08.2001

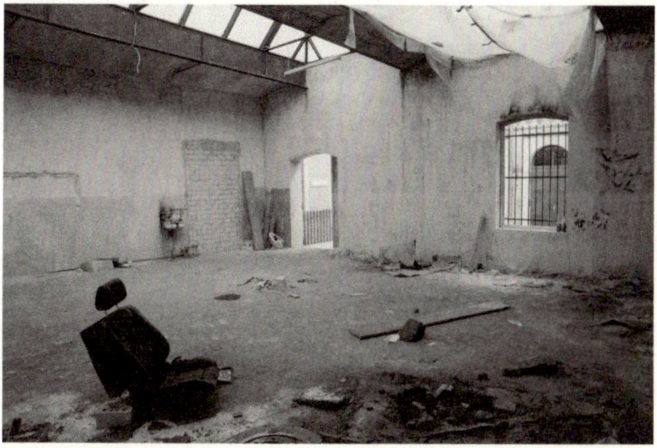

Pawel Althamer
30.04.2003 – 16.08.2003

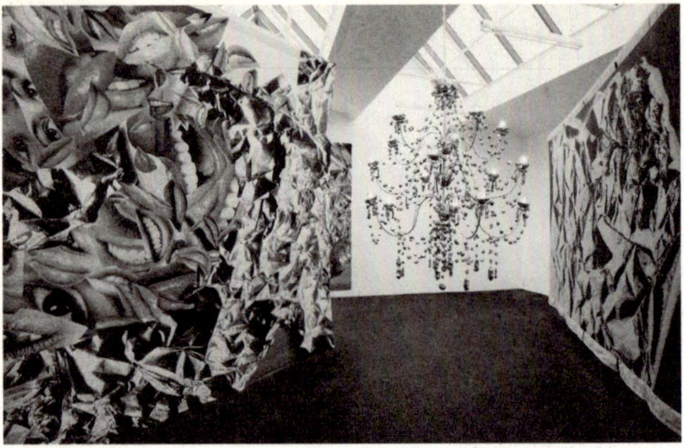

Pae White
Cotton Mouth
24.03.2005- 23.04.2005

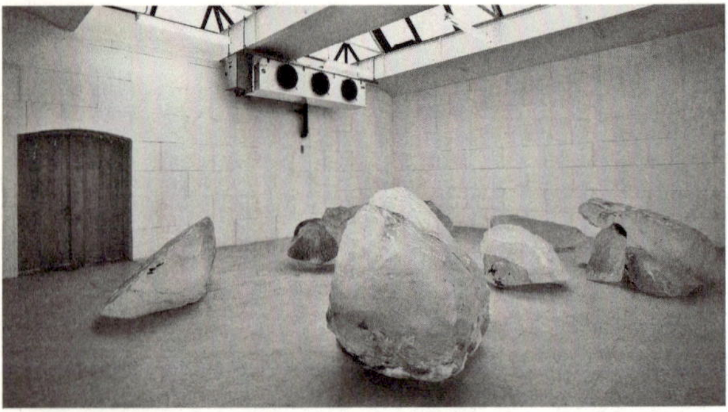

Olafur Eliasson
Your Waste of Time
24.03.2006- 22.04.2006

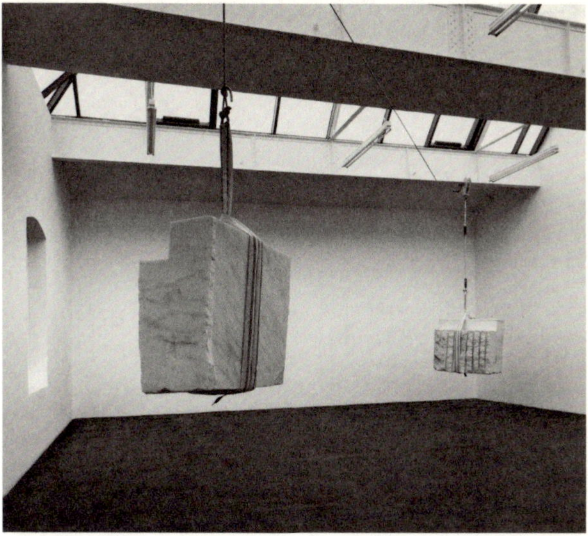

Simon Starling
The Long Ton
2.05.2009 – 27.06.2009

Installation views neugerriemschneider
All photos by: Jens Ziehe, Berlin
Courtesy: neugerriemschneider, Berlin

Franco Noero

GALLERIA FRANCO NOERO, TURIN

— When did you decide to become a gallerist?
I think I was fifteen at the time.

— What are your greatest qualities? What led you to become what you are now in the art world?
I find it easier to talk to you about my defects; I'm not that good at recognizing my strong points. But I know that I like working in a team, I'm extremely inquisitive, and I have the right mix of patience, obsession, and hysteria—and, yes, I would say tenacity, too.

— What led you to do the job you do?
Privilege. The absolute privilege of being able to work with an idea that comes up, believing in it, and fighting together with whoever created it to make it come true. This really is one of the most enjoyable challenges in the world. It's not like launching a product—we're talking about Art and Poetry, and it's incredibly sexy trying to base an economy on Poetry.

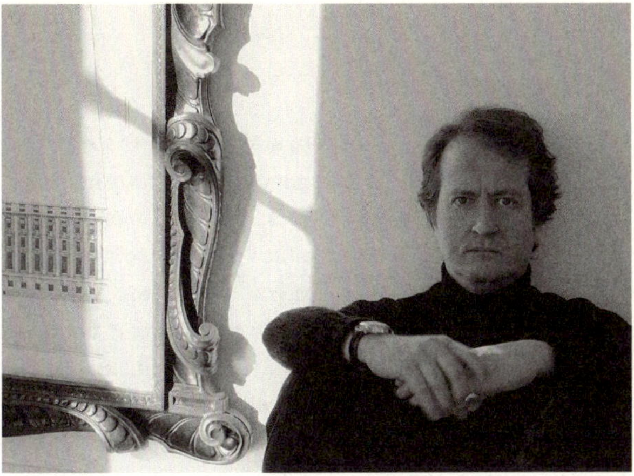

Franco Noero
Photo: Meris Angioletti

— The happiest moment and the most dramatic moment in your career?

I tend to forget the unhappy or dramatic moments very quickly. I just bury them. The happiest? I'm hoping it will come one day. I don't think I've had that many so far. But sure, when I see that mixture of pride and satisfaction in an artist before an opening, I'm really, really happy.

— Do you have particular fears?
Always. Every day. Fortunately.

— So, on the subject of fears: A few months ago you moved your gallery to a legendary building in Turin, built in 1840 by Alessandro Antonelli—who also designed the Mole Antonelliana, the architectural symbol of Turin. The building you moved into is known as the Fetta di Polenta, or "slice of polenta," because of its shape and color. It's a bizarre, trapezoidal construction, seven stories tall, and ending with a width of just fifty-four centimeters. Not exactly a "white cube"! Each floor is only a few square meters, and there's no lift. An absolutely absurd place for a gallery. Weren't you afraid it might not work? Is your hope that the building will encourage artists to make original projects?
Moving the gallery to the Fetta di Polenta was and still is a bet. But one that was dreamed up along with all the artists. And the result so far has been stunning. I want to create a real workshop of ideas. I believe in the gallery not just as a container but especially as a generator of ideas, and the Fetta di Polenta is responding to this perfectly. You could say it works extraordinarily well with the gallery artists' projects.

— What makes a good gallerist? And how do you become one?

You have to achieve a perfect balance between absolute respect for the artist's poetic vision, on the one hand, and the market, on the other. And you certainly need both commercial and intellectual honesty.

— Are you worried by changes in the role of the auction houses? I'm thinking of Damien Hirst's sale at Sotheby's, where he sold his works directly at auction rather than going through a gallery. He avoided paying fifty percent of his sales to a gallery owner, and sold his work at auction prices rather than the lower gallery ones. Don't you think this action will have consequences for the art world?
Initially I did, but now I don't. It was a long time ago—since September 2008, the world, and our world with it, has changed at least two or three times, and not through the merits or demerits of Damien Hirst (whom I've never had the good fortune of meeting personally). But I don't think Hirst would have become what he is today without a traveling companion like Jay Jopling, who was mad enough to buy him a five-meter-long dead shark in 1991.

— Will the gallery owner always be useful for the artist and collector?
Yes, certainly. If I didn't think so, I would leave this business.

— Five pieces of advice for someone starting a collection?
Just one: Buy out of love, not just as an investment.

— What should a collector never do to you (apart from not paying)?
Something like buying in June, paying the following January, and then selling at auction in February. And expecting to go to dinner with you the day before the auction. I promise you, it really happened.
Apart from this anecdote, if I see that a collector is purchasing solely for speculative purposes, I always tend to offer him what I think is least important. Automatically, and almost unconsciously. Let's be clear, the market is hugely important and plays a key role: Someone who buys is investing money, and you should never lose sight of this aspect. But I've always noticed that when a collection is not based on calculations but is built up with sensitivity, the most extraordinary economic results come in the medium to long term.

— What do you appreciate most in a collector?
Respect for the work, both before and after purchase. Which basically means respect for the artist and for what one can and cannot attain.

— We're going through a really tough economic crisis. How do you view this period? Do see any positive aspects in it?

Lots. Once the speculators are out of the way, there will be room for those who are devoted to the idea of building a collection. In the past two or three years, some prices were at fever pitch. I think that it will mainly be the artists and galleries who encouraged this frenzy who'll pay the most. There will be a clean sweep and a chance that Poetry, which I love talking about, can at last assert itself and grow. It will certainly be very tough for everyone, but I'm sure we'll come out stronger. Those who have aimed and who continue to aim for quality will, I think, have a chance to consolidate their position.

— Is it true that there are differences between Italian and foreign collectors? It seems that Italians always ask for a discount, as a matter of principle. Does that mean others don't?
Everyone asks for a discount. I know some French and Belgians who are even more brazen than many Italians when it comes to asking for discounts. Italian collecting is extraordinary, and not just now. In the great international galleries, there's almost always someone who can communicate in Italian. One wonders why.

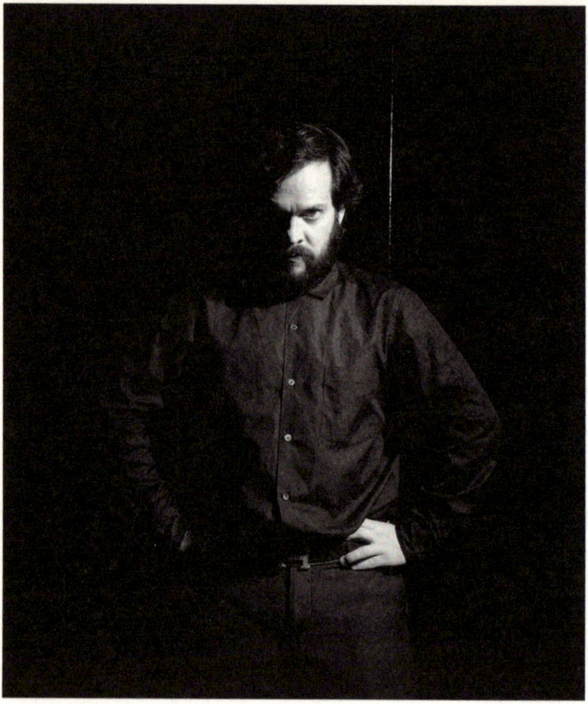

Javier Peres
Photo: Robert Brecko

Javier Peres

PERES PROJECTS, BERLIN / LOS ANGELES

— Javier, you have a background as a lawyer. How did you get into art, and why?

I have been interested in art since I was a child. I was surrounded by art from an early age and visited museums ever since I was a kid. In fact, many of my best childhood memories are of museum visits. My interest in art continued to grow and grow through my teens, when I started to collect drawings and some paintings by outsider artists as well as some modern artists, which my grandparents helped me acquire or gave me as gifts. I took a lot of art history courses in college, but my major was international politics and law, mainly because I already knew a good amount about art history and knew that I would keep learning more on my own, and I wanted to study something a bit more "practical" (my parents' word, not mine).

— You grew up in Cuba, and you come from a well-to-do Spanish family. Your paternal grandparents Josefa and Mario purchased art for decades, creating a collection that includes works by El Greco, Goya, Picasso, and many others. Now you spend most of your time in Berlin. What have you brought with you from Cuba, from your grandparents, and from your past?
Oh gosh, this is a tough question. I like to think that I live in the present, but of course the past informs us in many ways. I am very interested in history and in how history is made—this is important to me. I have pretty limited memories of my time in Cuba, so if there is anything that I took from living there, I am not too aware of it. From my grandparents, I think I inherited my interest in art and in collecting art.

— You initially opened a gallery in San Francisco, then one in Los Angeles, and another in Berlin. You immediately made a name for yourself in the art world. Why do you think that is?
Well, I hope it's because I show good artists and because I work hard.

— You told the *New York Observer* that you would never invest your money in art because it's not a good investment. Yet you entered the art world as a collector, and you're still buying. How many works do purchase for your collection each year?

I often lie to the press, giving answers I think the particular interviewer wants to hear, or I state things in a way that welcomes misunderstandings or multiple meanings. I am not entirely sure why I do this, other than because I think it is funny to see something you made up in print. Anyhow, that was the case when I said this at that time. I think art can be a great investment, whether in monetary terms or in personal satisfaction, for example. I buy as much art as I can, I don't know the exact number of works per year because it is constantly changing, and it really depends on what is available at any given time. But I would say fifty or so works a year would be a good guess. I should look into this; thanks for asking me the question.

— How did you meet Terence Koh? You have a close association, and you share a space in New York, the Asian Song Society. Tell me a bit about what you call the "New New School of New York."
Terence and I met through filmmaker Bruce LaBruce, I met several great people via my relationship with Bruce—Dan Colen, Dash Snow, Agathe Snow, and several others from that crew. I forget what I called it, but I don't think it was exactly what you said. But certainly, in my generation, there has been an incredible amount of creative energy coming out of New York, a level that has not, in my opinion, been

there for some time, maybe since the late 1970s or early '80s. This group of artists take the city as a great source of inspiration, they swear by its dirt, grit, and promise of a better tomorrow. I think it is an exciting scene, and I have really enjoyed working with and learning from all the New York–based artists whom I represent, or whom I have shown over the past six years.

— How do you choose your artists? Do you have a network of advisers you trust, or do you do it alone?
I do it totally alone, by and large. But it has always been a very organic process for me, meeting one person has led to another and then another.

— You once said that money is useful, but it doesn't count for much; what matters is the history of art. Have you yourself entered the history of art?
I think I have a long way to go before I enter the history of art, and I am not sure that this will ever really happen. My objective is to influence art history by the choices I make, by the artists I choose to represent and champion, that is what matters to me—not so much me personally being historically significant. When I am dead and long gone, I don't care if anyone remembers me, and they are unlikely to do so, but I do want them to still be discussing a Dan Colen painting, a Dash Snow photo, a Terence Koh

sculpture, a Bruce LaBruce film, an Agathe Snow installation, a Joe Bradley painting, a Mark Flood collage, a Dan Attoe painting, a Kirstine Roepstorff collage, an Assume Vivid Astro Focus installation, and so on. You know what I mean?

— What do you think about the present economic crisis? Do you agree with those who say it will make the art world more interesting and ethical?
The present economic crisis sucks. There is nothing I like about it, and I personally hate the notion that poverty makes art better or that it makes better artists. Great artists should be rewarded and reap the benefits of the fruit of their labor. In the past six or so years, artists started making a bit more money, maybe even more money than they had ever had before, and for some reason certain people, and certain critics and collectors, in particular, all of a sudden became offended because what had always been a "poor underclass" was experiencing some wealth. I really hate this hypocrisy, and it is unfortunate that we are now living in these messed-up economic times.

I am of the opinion that life is to be enjoyed and that one should seek pleasure whenever possible. Life is very uncertain, and the good things can end any minute. Therefore, I find it natural to celebrate and enjoy myself whenever possible, and I don't think this is something that the world economy will alter. It can, and has, made me think twice about where I put my money, and what I support and what I don't. We have taken steps to prepare ourselves for the current climate, but I am pretty hopeful that things will get better in the not-too-distant future. I think they have already started to get a bit better, certainly better than they were last fall. One more thing: Anyone who thinks that I throw the ultimate lavish art party has not been to that many parties!

— Let's close on a lighter note: What was your best instinct ever? The decision that changed your life. And is there one you wish you had never made?
I think I have great intuitions and terrible ones every day, but they usually have more to do with my personal life than with my business life—so I'll spare you the details!

Francesca Pia

GALERIE FRANCESCA PIA, ZURICH

— Francesca, you opened your first gallery in Berne in 1990. Did you have any previous experience as a gallery director?

I had no experience as a gallery director at the time. My background was art school and jobs in two internationally renowned galleries in Zurich.

— How did you choose your artists when you started? Did you have any advisers back then?

I knew many artists, such as Terry Fox, before I started the gallery; other artists I discovered while traveling for research, like Thomas Hirschhorn in 1990.

— Which of your exhibitions from the 1990s do you think was the most important?

Perhaps Peter Fischli & David Weiss in 1992.

— I can imagine. What have you learned from your relationship with these two great artists?

They influenced my view on a particular Swiss consciousness. Of course, I got a lot of attention and developed new relationships with curators and museum people, which inevitably influenced my standards in Berne.

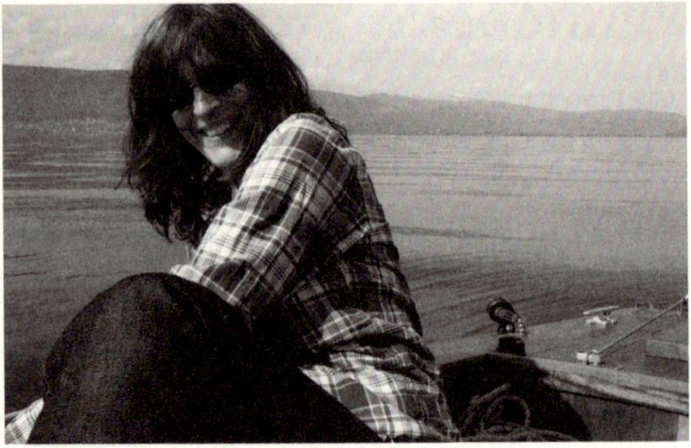

Francesca Pia

— Switzerland is a small country that plays a large role in contemporary art right now—a magnificent Kunsthalle; top museums, private foundations, and private galleries; and Art Basel, the most important art fair in the world. What lies at the heart of this success? Is it the result of a few influential people, or wider government initiatives and tax policies?
During World War I, Switzerland became a refuge for many artists, and the Dada movement was founded in Zurich. These events led to a positive climate for contemporary art, and an openness to it. At the same time, Swiss industrial families (e.g., Hahnloser, Reinhard, and later Oeri, to name a few) were pioneer collectors, which, of course, influenced the museums. New movements in the '60s with people like Harald Szeemann, and the magazine *Parkett* in the '80s,

encouraged a new form of dialogue between Europe and America. And yes, federal grants and generous acquisition policies also contribute to the promotion of contemporary art in Switzerland.

— What do you love about your work as a gallery owner, and what would you be happy to do without?
Of course, I love my communication with artists. I would be happy to spend more time on individual concepts and less on administrative work.

— What do you think ought to disappear forever from the world of art?
Speculation.

— Some people say that Italian collectors are brilliant, that they've got intuition and passion—but also that they have the bad habit of always and insistently asking for discounts. In your experience, is this true? Does that mean that other collectors don't ask for discounts?
The one Italian collector I know is indeed brilliant. It's not just the Italians who ask for discounts. I am very much looking forward to getting to know more Italian collectors, and this is why I'm coming to Turin. It would be wonderful to start a relationship with Italian collectors, as I have always loved being in this country for various and obvious reasons.

— What's the environment like in Berne? What do you think is missing from the arts there?
Berne's Kunsthalle presents historically important shows, and there are often interesting exhibitions in various innovative institutions. But by the turn of the millennium, Zurich had become an important city in the global world of contemporary art, and this meant it was necessary that I move there—for the careers of our artists and for the gallery itself.

— So in 2007 you moved the gallery to Zurich. What was that like?
I had a very good start, having had many contacts for years, and was well received by the art scene.

— How are you coping with the international crisis? Do think it might have a positive effect on the art market?
At first, I was very uncertain about the future of my gallery, but now I don't see much change personally. I am very happy to be allowed to talk more honestly about financial worries. It brings us all more together.

— What advice would you give to a young collector today?
The same as always: look and read.

Gregor Podnar

GALERIJA GREGOR PODNAR, BERLIN / LJUBLJANA

— You started your career as a curator. What is your educational background?
I graduated from the University of Cologne, where I studied art history, ethnology, and history of Eastern Europe. I finished my studies in 1997, but I had been working as a freelance curator since 1993.

— Before opening your gallery, you were director of the Galerija Škuc in Ljubljana. Are there many serious collectors in the country today?
Between 1996 and 2003 I was the artistic director of the Galerija Škuc in Ljubljana, an art space established in 1978 that was never involved in the art market. In 2001, I decided that we should take part in art fairs, and the following year we were in Liste in Basel. That was an important starting point for creating international interest, but locally, the growth of the contemporary art collector base has been slow. I opened Galerija Gregor Podnar in 2003, and I do have three or four good collectors. But there isn't a tradition of collecting contemporary art.

There is, however, an international-level collection by Igor and Mojca Lah, and young galleries have started going to art fairs, too. The Ministry of Culture recently started supporting participation in art fairs, similar to Austria, but there is still a long way to go before we have a well-structured art market in Slovenia. One cannot invent collectors; running a gallery is a long educational process. Slovenia will always be a small market, as its population is only two million people. But despite opening a gallery in Berlin two years ago, I decided to keep my space in Ljubljana as a long-term investment.

— What are the most interesting centers of contemporary art in Slovenia?
The most interesting one is the Moderna Galerija, in Ljubljana, the national museum of modern and contemporary art. In the mid-1990s, it established an international reputation as an important art center in Eastern Europe, in large part due to the tremendous efforts of its director, Zdenka Badovinac. The museum has a substantial collection of Eastern European art, mainly conceptual art, that unfortunately has not been in permanent display. The institution has recently lost some of that thrill of the '90s, but it is still one of the most active public spaces. Others include Mestna Galerija in Ljubljana and Likovni Salon in the city of Celje.

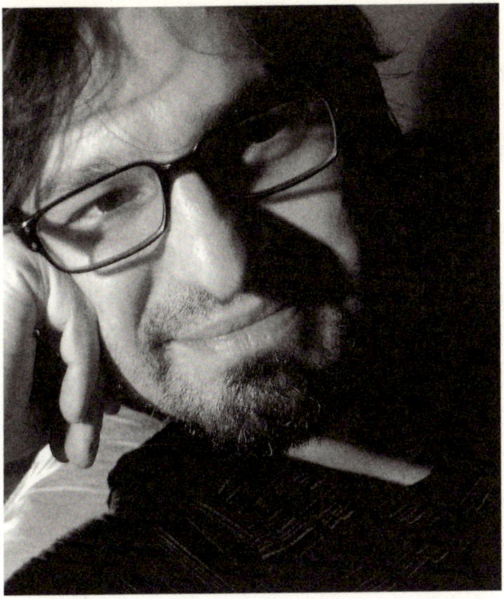

Gregor Podnar

There are also a number of galleries that are primarily publicly funded: Galerija Škuc, Galerija P74, Galerija Kapelica, Galerija Ganes Pratt, and a few others outside Ljubljana in Maribor, Murska Sobota, and Piran. But in general, the situation is a bit unexciting right now, so I hope that private initiatives—such as the newly established Academy of Visual Arts in Ljubljana—will help to free young artists and curators from what is still a very traditional and parochial art scene.

— How much of the gallery's sales take place at art fairs, and how much comes through your gallery?
The majority are connected to art fairs, especially to Art Basel and Frieze. Most of the best collectors are present at art fairs, but from time to time, they come to the gallery for the exhibitions.

— Your gallery opened in 2003, as an offshoot of the nonprofit Association DUM. What does the association do, and why did you choose that context for the gallery?
In Slovenia, the legal form of an association is very convenient for business in the arts. The other two members of DUM work in the visual arts and dance/theater. In the long term, it is better to open a regular company, but this kind of organization is good for the first few years of operation, especially when there's limited cash flow.

— What prompted you to move premises in 2005?
In 2003, I opened my first gallery premises in the small town of Kranj, half an hour by car away from Ljubljana. I could not afford the rents in Ljubljana at that time. It was a nice 190-square-meter space in a rundown industrial zone, and a very exotic start for the gallery in the middle of nowhere. Then, in the summer of 2005, I found a good gallery space in the center of Ljubljana.

— In October 2007, like many other gallery owners, you opened a branch in Berlin. Why was that?

Ljubljana is a small city with only around 270,000 inhabitants and, as I mentioned, with a relatively undeveloped art market, so I was looking for another city to open a second gallery. In 2006, Claes Nordenhake asked me if I wanted to join the gallery house at Lindenstrasse 34/35 in Berlin's Kreuzberg area. For some years now, Berlin has been attracting collectors from all over, so that was the main motivation to come to Berlin.

— What advice would you give to a young collector of contemporary art?

I believe it is important to communicate with other collectors and to travel to the galleries of the artists one is interested in and not only to observe their works at art fairs. And if you get good curatorial advice or are convinced by the work of an artist who has no gallery representation yet, you should go for it. It will help the artist to continue and to find the right gallery.

Eva Presenhuber

GALERIE EVA PRESENHUBER, ZURICH

— Between 1989 and 1997 you ran Galerie Walcheturm in Zurich turning it into one of the most important contemporary art spaces in Switzerland. How did this come about? And what had you done before?
Running Galerie Walcheturm was great. I started with no program and little money—just a small amount coming in from members, as it was kind of a club of art lovers and their friends. My first show was with Markus Geiger, a Swiss artist whom I knew from Vienna. I'm Austrian, and I studied art at the Hochschule für Angewandte Kunst in Vienna in the mid-1980s. Some of the very first artists I exhibited were artists based in Vienna or whom I'd known at art school—people like Gerwald Rockenschaub, Franz West, Ugo Rondinone. Later on, I was able to get in touch with Peter Fischli and David Weiss, as well as with Jean-Frédéric Schnyder, artists who were well known and whom I admired. And Beat Streuli joined the gallery around that time, 1989 to 1992. During that period I also went to New York and visited

galleries there. I was very fond of the work of Sue Williams and Karen Kilimnik, so I made contact with their New York gallery, 303, and owner Lisa Spellman. Soon afterward, I put on shows with these two great artists at Walcheturm. At that time, I was also organizing readings and concerts and lectures at Walcheturm, because I liked being involved with different kinds of cultural production—Hans Ulrich Obrist gave a lecture, Pipilotti Rist played with her band, Isabelle Graw lectured. Up to 1998, before I went into partnership with Hauser & Wirth for some years, I had already represented thirteen artists: Angela Bulloch, Candida Höfer, Peter Fischli & David Weiss, Urs Fischer, Maria Eichhorn, Douglas Gordon, Karen Kilimnik, Hugo Markl, Gerwald Rockenschaub, Ugo Rondinone, Jean-Frédéric Schnyder, Beat Streuli, Franz West, and Sue Williams.

— In an interview in *Artforum* in April 1998, you said that your vision of the gallery had always been somehow idealistic, and that you try to distinguish between art and pseudo-art. What do you mean by that?

I think being able to choose the right artists is a matter of knowledge, experience, and moral. Looking at what I said eleven years ago, I would say that I still have the same opinion, and my ethics have not changed. It's just like that.

— In the same interview, you state that you were helped and inspired early on by two Swiss artists, Ugo Rondinone and Urs Frei. They were very young at the time and had just finished art school. What was it that they taught you?

Ugo Rondinone, especially, had a big influence on me, and he still does. He's a great artist and a great curator, too. The show he curated last year at Palais de Tokyo, "The Third Mind," was a big success; it didn't drop names, just included great work. I was also influenced later on by Fischli & Weiss, Franz West, Dieter Roth, and Urs Fischer. Basically, every artist has influenced me. I love to become older with the artists I am showing, so I like to be loyal and be treated loyally.

— Urs Fischer is one of many young talents you've discovered. How did you meet Urs, and what convinced you to work with him?

I met Urs in 1994, and we put on our first show together in 1995. You could already feel the energy in his very early works, and his great spirit and intelligence.

— In 1998, you opened the Hauser & Wirth 2 gallery, which later became Hauser & Wirth & Presenhuber. Why did you leave Galerie Walcheturm? And have you ever considered working at a museum or institution?

You've done your research! I entered a business relationship with Hauser & Wirth in 1998. Changing the gallery name twice probably meant I was not really comfortable—and they probably were not either. I have never thought about working in an institution. My pleasure is in working on the success of artists, and I also enjoy building up great collections in a more direct way than would be possible at a museum. Independence is also important to me.

— You've been working in the art world for twenty years now, without ever putting a foot wrong. Or perhaps you've made some mistakes, too?
Everybody makes mistakes. I should probably have married a rich man.

— Philosopher Karl Popper says that luck is an important factor in success. Would you agree? Do you think you've been lucky?
I think it is all about meeting the right people at the right time and working hard. You can easily lose everything again if you take your luck for granted.

— With all your experience, what advice would you give to a young person who wants to open a gallery today?
Open a gallery if you have friends who are great artists and who want you to be their dealer.

Silvia Dauder

PROJECTESD, BARCELONA

— I read that you're a biologist, and that you also once worked in advertising. That's a strange background for a gallery owner! How did a biologist fall in love with art?

You are right, it may sound rare, but it is perhaps not such a bad combination, if you think about it. The years I devoted to biology gave me very good training in work methodologies and certain research skills. I also learned to deal with a lot of information and ideas. I was not so much in advertising, but I did work in film production with a top photography director. This gave me an opportunity to learn how to organize work, collaborate in a team, and pay attention to details, which are all very important. I find the experience in both fields very useful, formative, and interesting to apply in my current profession.

The decision to start an art gallery was not sudden. It took years to develop, and it was a very gradual process. I have always been interested in art, ever since I was a teenager. I used to spend hours in museums, not even knowing why. Before I decided to study biology, I thought of art history. So in a way I had never been removed from art, quite the contrary. I also think that the fact that I started the gallery without any working experience in the field was crucial for defining the identity of ProjecteSD. I think it was very good to come from a fresh, unpolluted perspective. I should add, there are other gallerists with degrees in science, and a few good artists as well.

— It can be rather risky to open your own gallery without first cutting your teeth working for someone else. What sort of difficulties did you encounter?
I found all sort of difficulties, but I guess I had and still have the strength to go through with it. There's a certain amount of naïveté at the beginning, which I think is necessary. And then you start seeing how complicated everything is. The biggest difficulty was not having a list of clients, without a doubt. But I find it a lot more challenging to move on, once you have set certain standards. People expect a lot from me now, and there is no way back.

— You work with a number of young Spanish artists. How do you select them? Do you have advisers?
I do not have advisers. Of course, you get to know more and more professionals, and there is an exchange of information, but I make my own decisions. It's the only way for me. If I make mistakes, it's my responsibility alone. I base my selections on the quality or potential of the work, and, of course, if the work and/or artist makes sense in the gallery context.

I never choose an artist for commercial reasons. I guess this is obvious if you take a close look at my program.

— Why did you open a gallery in Barcelona? The contemporary art market in Spain is basically in Madrid these days, or am I wrong?
Why not in Barcelona? I live here, and when I started the gallery, I did not consider moving to a new city. My program, my business, was never conceived to target just the local audience. I do not only have Barcelona-based clients; I sell to clients outside Barcelona and abroad. And with institutions, it is the same. For a young contemporary art gallery today, with an international program, it's a mistake to think locally. Maybe I would make more money in Madrid, but not in the long run, I think. It all depends on the networks you develop, so geographical distances do not matter so much. But, yes, Barcelona is tough, if you compare it with other European cities.

— Barcelona does have important institutions, such as MACBA, Museu d'Art Contemporani de Barcelona. What kind of relationship do you have with museums in the city? Can you briefly describe the art scene in Barcelona?
I do have an active relationship with institutions like MACBA. They follow my program and artists and have been supportive of ProjecteSD. And I think I support

them as well. I find it very difficult to describe the art scene in Barcelona, because it is not well structured and defined and probably not strong enough. I think that there are a few taboos that all of us should be able to overcome. There is not enough efficient communication among the different agents in the art scene—artists, collectors, galleries, institutions. There are a few good artists, but for some reason, certain types of art practices are chosen (and not necessarily the best ones) in order to play in the big leagues. We also have a serious educational problem at the art schools. They are not demanding and active enough; their capacity for exchange with international colleagues and centers is minor. No one debates this. And the same goes for artists and galleries—the interest in trying out new things and taking real risks is very limited. There is enough money but not enough good collectors, and behavior is very conservative, in general, not only among the bourgeoisie. To go beyond what is expected is very difficult in Barcelona. I think this is one of the reasons why ProjecteSD is starting to stand out. I do offer different views and unexpected names, in quality exhibitions.

— Who are the people who collect art in Spain? Are their numbers increasing? How is the art system changing in Spain?

The private collectors are lawyers, big corporations, architects, designers, doctors, gallerists, millionaires with no profession. And then we have art buyers, but these are not collectors. Like everywhere else I guess. The numbers of collectors are slowly increasing, but we are not in a good time for expansion now—although maybe it is not a bad time to start a good collection.

The art system in Spain is not changing; I would say, rather, that it is starting. There is not enough background or tradition for change yet. If too much happens too fast, you crash. But it may be good to crash if you survive and keep moving in a calmer direction. I have hope.

— How much of your sales come from international fairs and how much from the gallery itself?

I do not like art fairs, but I need them. Not only for the sales—a lot of the fairs I did last year were not exactly super successful in terms of sales, but they bring contacts, and it is a good exercise to present the gallery. Fairs offer exposure and publicity as well. You know, if I had not done Artissima last year, or if you had not liked my booth, this interview would not be happening. If you are not in art fairs, you do not exist—and that's sad. The real work of the galley is at home, not in the art fair, but I guess the world is like this now. You just have to find your own niche.

Lukasz Gorczyca and Michal Kaczynski

GALERIA RASTER, WARSAW

— You both have a background as critics and curators. Where did you study, and how did you get interested in contemporary art?

We both studied art history at the University of Warsaw, but we had met before, at a math-oriented high school, we were among a handful of pupils who had completely different interests from the rest of the school. It was back then that we became involved in art. We started as teenage poets, then moved on to the visual arts. We made drawings and organized our own exhibitions in glass-cases those were our first galleries. Like a number of our colleagues, our first contact with contemporary art came with the "Arsenal '88" exhibition in Warsaw, a grand festival of young Polish art organized in a former fair hall. Back then, we did not realize that the project was politically controlled by the Communist authorities and boycotted by the great majority of eminent artists. It was sort of a peculiar, negative initiation, but it was through this propaganda that we learned about the existence of a thing called "contemporary art."

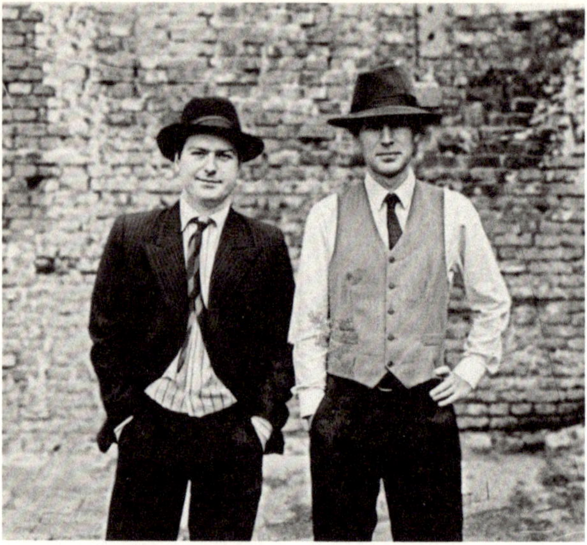

Michal Kaczynski/Lukasz Gorczyca
Photo: Zbigniew Libera

— Poland has long had a flourishing art scene. How did the end of the Communist regime affect contemporary art in Poland? In your opinion, who are the postwar Polish artists who have influenced the younger generations?

What changed in 1989 was, first and foremost, expectations toward art. Obviously, those expectations shifted toward new art, which would describe the new political situation. Postwar Polish art can be seen to maintain a continuity with modern art reaching back to before World War II, as seen in the careers of Henryk Stazewski and Tadeusz Kantor. Polish art of the 1950s–80s kept more or less within international (Western) standards. We had, and we still have, a great number of outstanding individuals (such as Andrzej Wroblewski, Alina Szapocznikow, Roman Opalka, Edward Krasinski, KwieKulik, Miroslaw Balka, Zbigniew Libera), who developed all kinds of contemporary trends, from Informel through to Conceptual art, to mail art and neo-expressionist painting.

Poland was lucky enough to be the country in the Soviet bloc that was set forth as an example that Socialism benefits contemporary art. So, in comparison with such countries as Czechoslovakia or Hungary, Poland enjoyed relative liberalism in this field. However, certain artistic approaches were marginalized in favor of those that seemed harmless to the authorities; for example, work that focused on self-contained artistic reflection was promoted over that which had overtly political content. Also for political reasons, a number of outstanding artists never received the chance to take part in the international art circuit—the KwieKulik duo were even deprived of their passports—an opportunity that is natural to artists of the younger generation.

In the second half of the 1990s, the infrastructure of art in Poland began to change as private galleries and foundations began cropping up. In recent years, the public sector has been developing, with new public institutions and museums of contemporary art. Wroblewski, Ewa Partum, Jurry Zielinski, Wladyslaw Hasior, KwieKulik, Jan Swidzinski, Natalia LL, Józef Robakowski—these artists are of crucial importance to a number of artists and others in our generation, although they are not necessarily known abroad.

— Artist Cezary Bodzianowski has described his time at Warsaw's Academy of Fine Arts as fundamental to his development. In his opinion, the driving creative force in '80s was the artist and teacher Marek Konieczny, who was later accused of corrupting his students and banished from the academy.

By the '90s, when we were students at the university—located across the street from the Academy of Fine Arts—nothing particularly interesting was taking place there. The academy, like the other art schools in Poland at the time, was an extremely conservative school, and, frankly speaking, it either hasn't changed at all, or it is changing very slowly. It always has a few good teachers, but these exceptions prove the rule. Bodzianowski and Piotr Uklanski were lucky to have been accepted to Konieczny's studio, but it was a unique and short-lived experience. Konieczny, like a number of other interesting artists, left after struggling with the conservative system of the institution.

— In 1995, when you were still very young, you launched *Raster*, a contemporary art magazine that became an online weekly in 2000. Was funding ever an issue? What is the magazine's editorial standpoint?

From the very beginning, we took the notion of self-organization and zine culture as a model—things that in Socialist times were labeled as "independent culture" or "the third circulation." Whenever we began working on any kind of project we never considered the source of funding. The money was almost unnecessary to us, as we learned to do everything either without it, or with minimal, studentlike expenditures. Such was the story with our first poetry volumes, and such was the story with *Raster*. We managed to obtain the first serious funding for it in 2003, when the whole undertaking was coming to an end. The paper edition of *Raster* cost us very little, and the internet weekly nothing at all: We wrote the majority of the texts ourselves, took the photographs, did the web design. We received server space for free, and at some point, a private sponsor gave us a digital camera. The money issue is related to our ecological philosophy—and this goes for the gallery, too: We do not print and send invitations by post, we only use e-mail, and recently also Facebook; we have neither a fax machine nor a telephone line. A lot of things turn out to be dispensable.

As for *Raster* magazine and its editorial line—from the start, we wanted to run an extremely subjective and sincere magazine, which was not difficult since we were doing it all just as a pair (although, of course, with a lot of help). We also, from the very beginning, had this ambition to speak as a "generational voice," and we were interested in finding young people with an outlook similar to ours. As far as editing style was concerned, *Raster* was something between an art zine, a literary quarterly, and a tabloid, but devoted to art. The magazine was completely flexible—every issue had a different form and layout. For the web version, our idea was to create easy access to a critical-information forum that would both stimulate and integrate the art scene. An important part of this approach was to react to the mass-media coverage of various phenomena in the domain of recent art, by exposing manipulations and abuses of various public institutions as well as the media themselves. The internet weekly was, immodestly speaking, our huge success. The vast majority of people in contemporary art in Poland would start their week by reading *Raster*.

— Some maintain that your magazine contributed to a renewal in critical language in Poland.

We think that *Raster* did indeed influence the way contemporary art was perceived, particularly by the younger generation, our peers. Speaking in corporate language, we seem to have produced good PR for contemporary art. It became a bit more popular and attractive in Poland. The language we used in *Raster* was, on the one hand, full of humor and irony, and on the other hand, it did not evade evaluation. On the contrary, we put a lot of effort into thoroughly criticizing all symptoms of conservatism, academicism, bureaucracy, and stupidity in contemporary art. We wrote a lot about bad art, and why, in our opinion, it is bad. In a sense, it was about creating a new system of values from scratch.

— What are the most important changes that have taken place in the Polish art scene in the past decade?
Fortunately, much has changed in the past decade. These changes are heading us in a predictable direction: the gradual professionalization of the contemporary art scene. This is good because operating standards rise, along with the quality of projects, exhibitions, educational programs, and artists' working conditions. Private galleries, foundations, and new public institutions have been emerging as well as collectors. One needs to remember that we really started at zero—when we opened our gallery in 2001, it was the first gallery in Warsaw with a regular exhibition program and a list of represented

artists, all young and emerging. In the past ten years, the attitude of officials and politicians toward art has also gradually changed. Now they seem more cautious, so as not to do something stupid; and they see that this field gives them quite a possibility to show off. Of course, this gradual evolution is accompanied by nostalgia, as the more professional our society becomes, the more difficult it is to find spontaneous and unexpected endeavors. So far, our effectiveness has lain in the capabilities of non-standard and innovative actions, which gave rise to such hybrids as *Raster*—part magazine, part private gallery, part a club of young intelligentsia, part a local culture house. Now, when the system kicks in, such freedom of action will be increasingly difficult to find. But one has to keep up an anti-system mode of thinking. Such was the spirit in which we developed, and this is what will—hopefully—protect us.

— In 2001, you opened the Raster premises. It's not just a gallery but an arts center with literary events, conferences, and concerts. In a nutshell, what exactly is your project about?
Raster is an accelerator of art and contemporary culture. We are interested in contemporary works in the field of nuclear physics, existentialism, visual perception, and political incorrectness as well as illusions and misconceptions. We exhibit and publish

works that are solid, liquid, or vaporous, in all languages, that affect all senses, as long as they touch the conscience and the crystallized image of reality. We introduce valuable art objects into the circuit and eliminate the surplus of artistic production by the physical destruction of cultural recycling. We are meticulous and inquiring—we are focused on the discovery and understanding of particles in order to obtain an image of the world in a higher resolution. Our task is to atomize the centers of power, develop thematic communities, and strive for the intellectual independence of each individual.

— What is your advice to a young person who wants to open a gallery?

First, find a partner who will help. Second, don't take too much advice, do what you think will be right. Third, do only what you are interested in.

Regina and Vladimir Ovcharenko

REGINA GALLERY, MOSCOW

— You opened your gallery in 1990, when Russia was emerging from seventy years of Communism and the Western art market was about to enter a period of great crisis. What do you remember of those days?

The Russian art market was completely absent, so we didn't have those problems here. But it was a time of great optimism, and all Russians—not just artists—found themselves without restrictions and thought that everything was possible.

— What are your and your husband's backgrounds? What did you do before you had a gallery?

Vladimir, my husband and the gallery's co-owner, had owned a business since 1988, and it required a lot of work. It was a time of experiments, in business, too.

— Between 1990 and 1993, artist Oleg Kulik was the director of the gallery. How did you meet him? Did you choose your artists with him?
It was a great cooperation. Oleg was a curator, or as he said, an "expositioner." Sure, we discussed all the projects together.

— Your program would suggest that a central aim has always been to support Russian artists. Is that correct?
It was only natural that we should support Russians—they are so creative, and we have supported each other. And there was not enough information about international art.

— In your opinion, what was the gallery's most important exhibition in the early years?
"Festival of Animalistic Projects" (1992); Ivan Chuikov's "The Theory of Reflection" (1992), and Oleg Golosiy's solo exhibition (1991).

— You also played an important role in bringing international art to Russia. The gallery presented "On Beauty," a 1996 group show curated by Dan Cameron, with the artists Gabriel Orozco, Mike Kelley, Rirkrit Tiravanija, and Mariko Mori, among others. How did that exhibition come about? Do you think it had an effect on the Russian art scene?

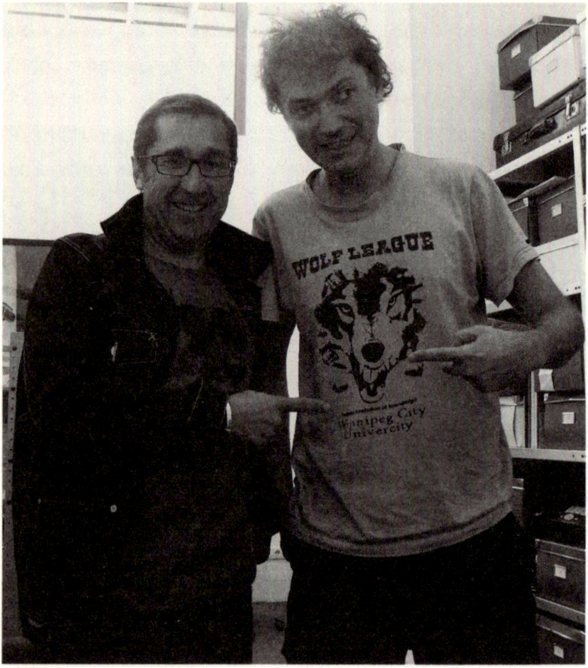

Vladimir Ovcharenko / Pavel Pepperstein

Optimism—optimism pushed us so hard! And it was crazy to do such expensive projects without any chance of covering the costs. But sometimes dreams can come true. It was the first show to be so significant in a private space in the 1990s. And it was unique until the end of the 2000s.

— Moscow has changed radically in the past twenty years. Is there something that you miss about the city as it was when you began? How would you describe Moscow today?

Moscow is getting so eclectic these days. A strange mixture of European and Asian things. The optimism disappeared, and glamour arrived.

— What are the main places devoted to contemporary art in the city today?

There are several places, which have been developed recently. There is Garage, managed by Dasha Zhukova, which hosts the big and expensive shows (Ilya Kabakov, Pinault's collection, the Moscow Biennale), and there is Winzavod, where all the best Moscow galleries are located. Red October is now trying to open more galleries in the center of Moscow.

— Organized crime is a huge issue in Moscow, although as an Italian, I shouldn't talk. Does it affect your gallery? What else would you like to change about Russia today?

Corruption—that's what we must fight against.

— Chinese collectors are rather conservative, and they generally tend to buy Chinese art. What sort of approach do Russian collectors adopt?

They start with Russians, but we have seen a lot of interest in international art over the past five years. And believe me, it's just the beginning. It will be a really serious market five years from now.

— How are you reacting to the current crisis? Is it economically worthwhile taking part in fairs these days?
We are long-distance players. We are using this difficult time to make our next move: We are working on opening the gallery in London and Kiev. Our participation in the best art fairs is part of our strategy.

— What advice would you give to a young collector who wants to start building a collection today?
Love art and buy what you love.

Sylvia Kouvali

RODEO, ISTANBUL

— Like many other young gallery owners, you studied art history. Where did you study, and how did you encounter contemporary art?
I studied art history and theory and philosophy of art. I studied first in Athens and then received my postgraduate degree in London, at Goldsmiths. Contemporary art has always been in my life through books and the museums and galleries I always visited with my family. My family's friends have always been artists.

— You worked for a number of years in Istanbul. which means you've seen some radical changes in the city's art world. As you see it, who has led the transformation and development of the Turkish art system over the past ten years?
I can only speak of the last five years, which is the time I have been in Istanbul. The developments are the result of a combination of individual efforts that somehow act separately from each other.

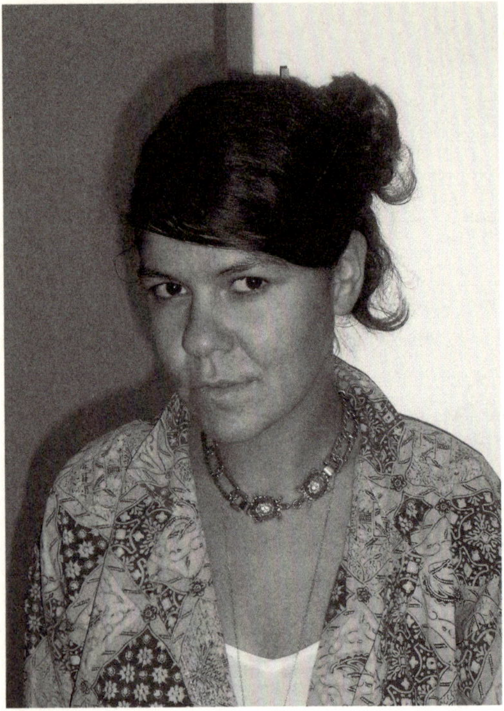

Sylvia Kouvali

It is first and foremost, artists who have been producing a certain kind of work at a certain time; meaning, at a moment that Turkey was entering the "art map," artists reacted to that in a positive way, and there was a certain first boom that somehow still haunts Turkish art production. At the same time, there were important people who surrounded and contextualized the moment and the work. Vasif Kortun, the director of Platform Garanti, has definitely been a leading figure. With the creation of Platform Garanti in 2001, things really started taking shape. Each biennial in Istanbul has had its own influence on the city, leaving its own marks. The one I experienced closely was the 2005 Istanbul Biennial, curated by Vasif and Charles Esche. Since then, new spaces have opened, such as Banu Cennetoglu's BAS, URA, and stuff in Hafriyat. A new wave of international people came and stayed.

— Who is the audience for contemporary art in Istanbul?
There is a different crowd for every institution, built throughout its history and shows.

— You initiated the public art project Yama in 2006. Can you describe it briefly?
Yama is a fifty-four-square-meter screen on top of the Marmara Pera Hotel, one of the biggest hotels in Istanbul, in a super central location. Yama was first

curated by me (2006–2007), then by Mark Aerial Waller (2007–2008). I worked with artists like Angelo Plessas, Giles Round, Jenny Holzer, Wael Shawky, Köken Ergün, Haris Epaminonda, and others; Mark showed works by Emre Hüner, Mark Leckey, Tobias Bernstrup, Tobias Collier, Fatma Ciftci, and more. Michelle Cotton and I co-curated the first group show, which ran in a random loop, with works by Mark Titchner, Paul Snowden, Babak Ghazi, Mustafa Hulusi, and Eva Weinmayr. For September, Johannes Fricke Waldhausen invited Jordan Wolfson. From now on, a curator will be invited to choose an artist. It's great!

— Your gallery, Rodeo, works with Turkish and international artists. How do you choose your artists?
I have been working with a small group of artists who come mainly from Turkey, Greece, and Cyprus. There is no straight policy, but I work with artists who inspire me. The list is growing slowly, and more interesting people are coming on board. There are elements of historicity and conceptual art and video that I find common between Rodeo's artists, and it is very exciting to see them all in group shows.

— How much of your annual turnover comes from Turkish collectors, and how much from collectors abroad?
95% international, 5% Turkish.

— Is there something you'd like to see come to Istanbul? Or something you wish would disappear?
I'm looking forward to seeing the new premises of Platform Garanti, and all that will bring to the city, and some new private museums and collections. I wish that the macho element that is dominant in this society, and has affected the art community, will gradually disappear. I would like to see more freedom and originality in shows, not just the usual suspects—the artists on all the young curators' lists.

— Turkey is an extraordinary country, both modern and traditional, international and insular, progressive in some ways while being economically and politically conservative. Do you think contemporary art can play a role in democratization?
I don't know so many countries in the region (including EU members) that are characterized by political and economic liberalism. Coming from Greece myself, and being a European citizen, I am so ashamed of how immigrants are treated and economic scandals are hidden under the table. Has contemporary art played a role in helping things to improve? I am not so sure. Galleries open in areas where immigrants are arrested daily and heroin is sold, and I don't see any improvement coming from the art communities.
But I know what you mean, and yes, in a small way, contemporary art can play a role in democracy.

But I think the art world thinks it's bigger than it is. Believe me, in Turkey it is tiny and can't do much, unfortunately.

— I've noticed that you often present solo shows at your stands in art fairs. I find this courageous and intelligent, but it's certainly risky from a commercial point of view. How are you dealing with the crisis?

I don't believe that the crisis will be as traumatic for galleries like Rodeo as it is for older and bigger galleries. For Rodeo, 2009 has been so much better than 2007 or 2008. I hope that the crisis will not worsen, for everyone's sake. On the other hand, some pause is only for the better—some introspection, reconsideration, and . . . fresh air.

Anna Schwartz

ANNA SCHWARTZ GALLERY, MELBOURNE / SYDNEY

— Anna, you recently opened a gallery in Sydney after running one in Melbourne for more than twenty years. What difference do you find in the art systems in the two cities? Is there a greater tradition of collecting in Sydney?
Although the gallery has only been in existence in Sydney for one year, I had held numerous exhibitions there in the past, in temporary spaces, and I have a close relationship with the many public galleries, where our artists have had high visibility. I have also worked with many Sydney collectors. In the end, Australia is one culture and one market. There is a lot of travel and communication between the two cities.

— The new gallery, restored by architect Tim Greer, is huge, and it's located in a former industrial complex known as CarriageWorks. Can you explain what makes this site so interesting?
In a city that is now so developed, it is really surprising to find this large, untouched, early industrial complex of buildings. The spaces, internal and external, are huge, and the physical experience is wonderful. Performance Space, which is also located there, presents interesting projects, and the Sydney Festival usually has a large presence at CarriageWorks in the summer.

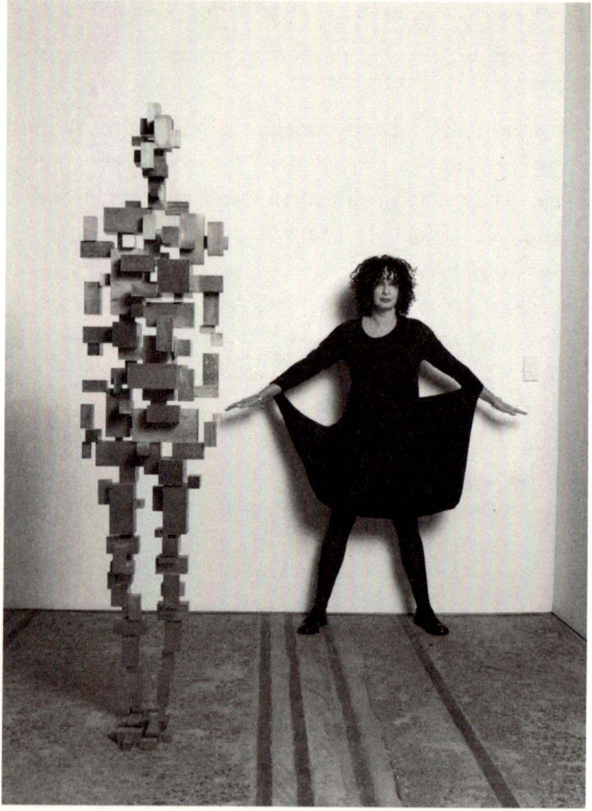

Anna Schwartz
Photo: James Cant @ The Artist Group
Artwork: Antony Gormley, *Sublimate XX*, 2008
Courtesy the artist and Anna Schwartz Gallery, Melbourne & Sydney

— How do you intend to use the enormous premises of the new gallery? Are you thinking of putting on curated exhibitions? Solo displays?

This gallery gives us the opportunity to present large-scale curated exhibitions and major projects by individual artists, which diversifies the art scene in the private galleries. We have already had a major show of artists working in neon, which included Joseph Kosuth, Tracey Emin, Pierre Huyghe, Kendell Geers, and Laurie Anderson. Our current exhibition, "Make a Scene," features three young Australian artists whose work is performative in very different ways.

— You've been running a gallery for a long time now, so you've probably witnessed the Australian art system change a great deal. How has collecting, for example, changed over the years?

The culture has grown and matured enormously since I opened a gallery twenty-seven years ago. The kind of art that we were showing was mainly the province of the museums then, but now there is a large and very committed number of collectors. Currently, there are a number of significant collections of international art.

— Australia is far removed from most of the art world. How does this distance affect the art scene there? Do you ever feel isolated?

Well, we travel easily and frequently. So we are present at most events and see everything as it comes up. The challenge is to encourage people from the rest of the world to come here. The Biennale of Sydney, the Asia-Pacific Triennial, and the Melbourne Art Fair attract collectors and curators, and they invariably continue to visit. I hope our exhibitions will provide an incentive for people to come as well. Once here, there is so much to see.

— What do you think about art fairs? Do you sell in Europe and the United States?
Art fairs are great for meeting people and for disseminating the work and ideas of the artists we work with. Yes, we sell in Europe and the US.

— Is there anyone in particular you feel you owe your fortune and success to?
The artists I have worked with, who have been so generous with their advice and their commitment to the gallery.

— Do you have any plans you haven't been able to put into practice yet?
I think I have lived my life by creating new objectives and trying to achieve them—so, yes, many. Now these are probably to extend and intensify what we have already established. I want to continue our publishing program, and there is a film I want to make.

— What kind of film?

A documentary kind of film about a remarkable art world personage.

— How would you advise a young person who's approaching the world of collecting right now?

Look at your own generation of artists, as their concerns—whether you initially realize it or not—will be relevant to you. Look at everything, but narrow your collecting activities at the early stages, establishing focused relationships with artists and galleries, so that you can learn about the work and its context.

— Let's end by starting from the beginning. Who is Anna Schwartz? What's your background? How did you end up in the art world?

I changed my profession from a university career and opened a gallery in 1982 after the death of my young husband, an artist. It seemed then to be the most useful and interesting life I could imagine. It is difficult at times, but I have been privileged to engage with the ideas and work of the most interesting and important artists of our day. I have great colleagues in both galleries, and with their participation, it has been very gratifying to see the gallery grow.

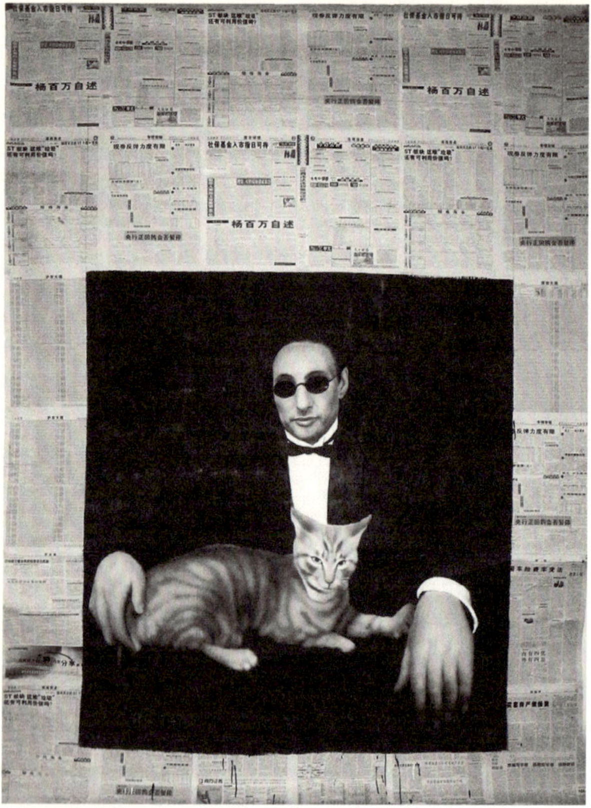

Lorenz Helbling

Lorenz Helbling

SHANGHART, SHANGHAI

— Lorenz, you have a fascinating past: You were born in Brugg, a little town in Switzerland, and your father and a brother are artists. You studied art history at Zurich University, and then Chinese and film in Shanghai in the 1980s. After working in film in Switzerland, you moved to Hong Kong and started working with the Plum Blossoms Gallery. By the mid-1990s you were back in Shanghai, where you opened the city's first contemporary art gallery. You put on your first exhibitions in the corridors of the Hotel Portman Ritz-Carlton. . . . Wow! Why Shanghai? Good intuition? Or just a lucky move?

It was a natural move to go back to Shanghai, where I'd spent my years of studies.

— You opened your gallery at a time when very little was known about Chinese art in Europe. I remember, for example, how surprising it was to see Chinese artists at the Venice Biennale in 1993 (Ding Yi, Li Shan, Yu Youhan and Sun Liang, from Shanghai alone) and very little else in the early 1990s. Would you ever have expected the phenomenal international success that these artists achieved just a few years later?

Not really—but on the other hand, living here in China in the '90s, I had trouble understanding people who looked at art in Paris, New York, London, etc., and thought they had seen all the art in this world. That work looked outdated, and it seemed logical to me that the category "international art" would soon include art from China.

— As I see it, the worldwide success of Chinese art, between 2000 and 2005, is a milestone in the history of art, or at least in the history of the sociology of art. Your artists began commanding sky-high prices within the space of just a few years. You now have three exhibition premises in Shanghai and one in Beijing, and you represent more than forty Chinese artists. Let me put it bluntly: Are you a millionaire? I think you are, although that was never what you were aiming for, at least at the beginning. Is that right?
I've never thought about whether I'm a millionaire or not. If there is money, it's reinvested in the artists and exhibitions.

— I don't want to ask you how China has changed, because your reply could fill an entire book. But I will ask you how your way of working has changed since you achieved your stunning success. Are you still having fun? Is there poetry in what you're doing?
Poetry is often at the beginning—luckily, or possibly unluckily, things are still at the beginning here.

— And how has your gallery changed? Were you besieged by speculators as interest in Chinese art grew? That must have influenced the mechanisms of your gallery.

Strangely, we are still working hard to find people who share our enthusiasm for the artists we are working with, to find people who are open and curious and also ready to put their money down if they see a work or an artist they believe in. Of course, for some of our artists that's easier now, and prices are higher, but we work all the time with new artists, and here we still need to do a lot of convincing.

Speculators: I've never much understood them, and they mostly keep away from the gallery. We are also pretty proud that only a few of the works we've sold have ever appeared in auctions.

— You were one of the first to show artists who became real stars, like Zeng Fanzhi, Zhou Tiehai, Yang Fudong, and Xu Zhen. How did you choose your artists?

"Don't be afraid to make mistakes" was a good piece of advice I got from Harald Szeemann at the beginning of ShanghART. I try to get an understanding of what the artists feel and are concerned with. Nobody knows how new art looks: We just need to be curious and open.

— What accomplishments are you particularly proud of?

That we really found great artists to work with, and we can work long term with them (or they with us).

— On the other hand, is there anything you wish you hadn't done?

Ten things every day—but happily, the pace of things is quick here, and they are forgotten quickly.

— Is the Chinese art market entering a period of normalization? Do you think China is going to go out of fashion?

The West often thinks everything depends on its attention and likes to see the world in terms of fashions (even better, of course, if they are created in the West). China is a country of more than a billion people and has one of the world's biggest economies, which is still growing fast, so it would be a strange thing to think that this might disappear in the next season like a miniskirt or whatever.

Which art works, which artists will stay? Here I am more skeptical: Many were hyped in the past solely by the auction houses, and the public was not that well informed (the art system and art infrastructure is still at the beginning, there are not enough museums, critics, etc., etc.). I think some artists may lose some of their luster, but many other more interesting ones will get the respect they deserve if the public pays more careful attention—as in every country. We really should get away from talking about "Chinese art" and start talking more about individual artists and their merits.

— One last question: Is there something particular to Chinese artists that sets them apart from those of the West?

There are many strong artists here, and to find common traits seems difficult to me. Some are in their twenties, some in their thirties, forties, or sixties; some live in big cities, some in faraway places; and so on. Perhaps there is one thing: Artists here don't tend to see themselves as happily standing in a corner—the whole world is important to them, and they know they live in a global world, and that the world is changing, so their position will change. There is no complacency, and no security, no matter how much success they have at the moment. It's better to be sensible, learn, and improve all the time. China is a great place for contemporary art.

Emily Sundblad

REENA SPAULINGS FINE ART, NEW YORK

— I have vivid memories of one of your first exhibitions, in 2004. It was a show of works by Josh Smith, you hadn't sold a thing, and the gallery looked kind of like a squat. I brought your only customer: a young Italian artist who bought a small picture. But within the space of a few years, Josh Smith became an international star, and you'd built up one of the chicest galleries in the world. Now, five years on, what do you think about all that has happened? Are you tired? Do still have hopes and ambitions? Projects you're excited about?

Yes, I remember. Gabriele Picco! We eventually sold all those paintings. Tired? Certainly not.

Hopes and ambitions and exciting projects? Of course . . . lots. New York is good right now. Whatever intensifies the city is most important to me. At the moment, we are planning K8 Hardy's debut show at Reena Spaulings. I'm excited about that!

— I've often had the idea that you feel rather ill at ease as Reena the star. Is that right? How have you dealt with the sensation caused by the Reena Spaulings project?

Hmm, it all depends on the context and what is actually happening. I feel most at ease as a hostess in the gallery. Or singing on a stage. I like controlling the context I am in, to some degree. But Reena Spaulings does not have a sole spokesperson. The gallery speaks for itself through the exhibitions we do and the artists we represent. When we do good shows it causes sensations.

— Reena Spaulings began as a character in a book by the collective Bernadette Corporation, then became a gallery, and then an artist. What is the next episode?
The gallery came first, in fall 2003. The book was published in January 2005 and coincided with the artist Reena Spaulings's first solo show at Haswellediger in New York. What's next? The movie, the sequel.

— When and why did you decide to open a gallery?
I needed a visa, and in order to get it, I had to rent a space. The cheapest one we could find was an old dress shop in my co-op neighborhood on Grand Street. It was only $1,500 a month. When I got the visa and could come back to the United States, the store was sitting there with a three-year lease. New York needed something. Chelsea was so boring. There was nowhere to go—only Maccarone Gallery had an interesting vibe sometimes. John Kelsey and

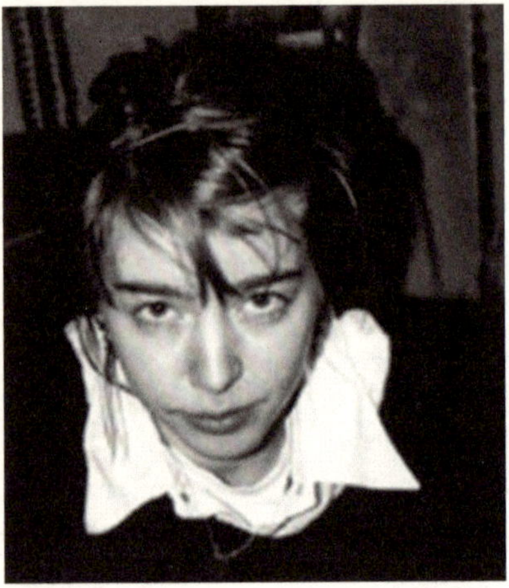

Emily Sundblad

I began talking with our friends. We started doing things in the space. First a party with top-shelf liquor donated by Jay Sanders. He'd received it as a gift from a collector. We screened the film *Daddy* by Niki de Saint Phalle and drank poppy tea. Then Agathe Snow had her first solo show. Then we ripped up a Michael Krebber catalogue and made a guerrilla Krebber show out of it. Then the Reena Spaulings Country Band was formed with Richard Maxwell. John translated *Tous les chevaux du roi* by Michèle Bernstein. Each month we gave away a new chapter, and it served as a program for the gallery, listing our activities.

— Some people think you're just playing a sort of game, that it's a pastime for bored kids. But you've introduced a whole range of interesting artists, such as Klara Liden, Josh Smith, Agathe Snow, Seth Price, Jutta Koether, K8 Hardy, Josephine Pryde, Claire Fontaine, and so on. How do you choose your artists?

An art gallery is a social phenomenon. Like New York, it is built on relationships. All the artists we show are our friends, and through friends you make new friends. A lot of the artists we show or have shown did not call themselves "artists" when we first started exhibiting them. We've never done a studio visit. Wait—once, with Nora Schultz.

Bored kids? You mean perhaps that there is an idea that we are not serious about what we do. That kind of dismissive judgment comes from confusion and the irritation that causes, I believe. There are so many dubious things in the mix: Art, to begin with. Art dealers who insist on also being artists. Collaborative work. Irregular hours. Powerful women. The gallery is messy sometimes. Being messy is still controversial.

— Do you think the Reena Spaulings project has earned you a place in the history of art? Do you ever wonder about this? Was this your initial aim?

The project began because it needed to happen, and we wanted it to. Yes, I think Reena Spaulings Fine

Art and Reena Spaulings have earned a place in the history of art. If you really want something recorded as history, though, you have to fight for it.

— I'd like to know what you think about the present financial crisis. Is it going to change your way of working? Do you agree with those who say the crisis will help flush out the system?
It is tedious and time-consuming to chase after people who owe us money, and we have to be more frugal now. It was scary when the crisis hit, and New York felt so sad. Now it feels better. I don't think hard times make for better people or improved ethics. But I've noticed interesting things happening in the city. Something about the style on the street is shifting. Maybe the monsters can come back. New York felt so antiseptic for a while.

— What are your personal hopes for yourself?
I really want to get a driver's license. But if I have an artistic, political aim, I guess it is to try to break down oppressive hierarchies and power structures. Or at least to show (myself and others) that they are not to be feared. This is especially important for women.

Marco Altavilla and Paola Guadagnino

T293, NAPLES

— Paola, T293 came into existence as a cultural association in 2001. I image that your apprenticeship the previous year, at the Centro di Documentazione e Archivio Giovani Artisti (Young Artists' Archives and Records Center) of the Associazione Viafarini in Milan, had quite an influence on your first project. When and why did you decide to turn the association into a gallery?

Initially, I had a burning desire to gather information about contemporary art, and the Viafarini archives were the perfect place for this. Since I was living near the library, I used to spend evenings reading catalogues and magazines, and during the day, I would sift through information about scores of artists. When I got back to Naples, I set up T293 and started a long period as a self-taught professional, and later turned the association into a gallery. It was thanks to the association that I was able to start reaching out to the public in Naples and acquiring work experience with artists. When I finished what

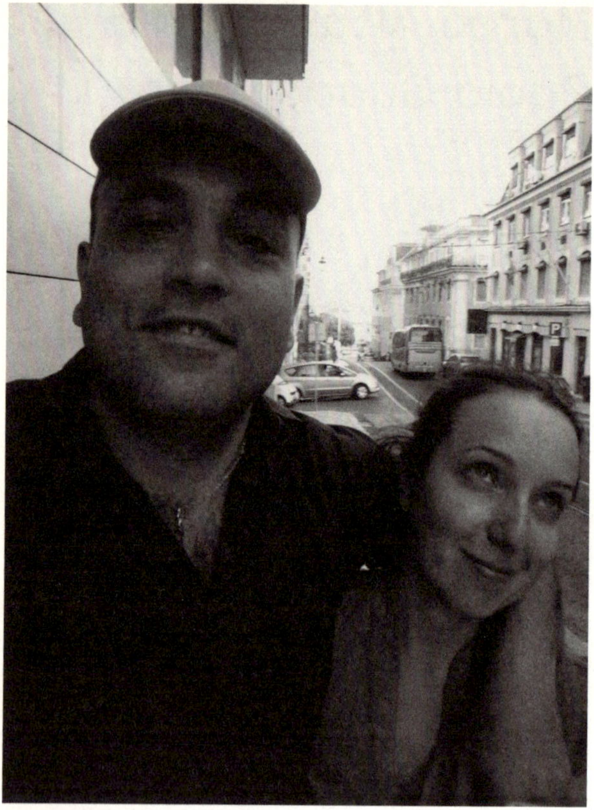

Marco Altavilla / Paola Guadagnino

I refer to as my “apprenticeship with myself,” I registered with the Chamber of Commerce.

— How much did your debut in the nonprofit sector influence the way you ran the gallery?
T293 started out as a cultural initiative, and only later turned into an entrepreneurial enterprise. The research and experimental aspects of an alternative space are still present in our work today. They have the same importance as the economic side that keeps us running, for they are an inexhaustible source of inspiration and knowledge. Then, of course, we need to transform them into top-quality decisions, and we’re working as hard as we can on this.

— Marco, you became co-director of the gallery in 2005, but you had worked previously as a critic and curator. Did you immediately adapt to your new role as gallery director? Was it difficult acquiring the mentality of a dealer?
The path that Paola was following wasn’t that different from my own, it was just that I didn’t have a fixed base. I would say I found my feet pretty quickly, mainly because I didn’t have to abandon a certain intellectual approach. Within a short time, I managed to complement her work with a management role that I don’t mind at all—just as I don’t at all mind the idea that a community of art lovers is building up around us.

— Paola, a few years ago you told me that you felt like leaving the city because of the social tension around you, but that in reality you would never quit.
For Marco and me, leaving Naples would mean not just abandoning a place and a culture but abdicating a political position that is very much part of our private and, especially, public approach. Basically, it would mean dodging a series of responsibilities. However difficult, contradictory, and anarchic it may be, Naples is, for us, a very tough but invaluable training ground, where every day we learn something from the countless variables it offers. This means we have to keep questioning our work, and we constantly have to work on finding solutions.

— Do you cooperate with the contemporary art museums and foundations in the city?
Our relationships with institutions in Naples are based on the fact that we all have the aim of promoting local contemporary art on an international level. T293, Fondazione Morra Greco, and Museo MADRE are deeply rooted in the old city. Although we have different pasts and ways of working, we show that it is possible to talk of local identity through the language and work involved in contemporary art. There has been a tendency to set up shop in the old part of the city, which is an unparalleled place not just in terms of its architecture, which is anything but tidy and antiseptic,

but also because of its interaction with a cultural and social world that brings together individuals and communities. T293 was the first to perceive the potential of the city center, and we are very happy that we were followed shortly after by an important foundation and a thriving museum.

— In your opinion, what are your finest qualities?
Tenacity, patience, curiosity, and intuition. But what we really share is our passion for art and artists, the way we are thrilled by something really new, something that still doesn't have a precise shape, and by trying to imagine the way it will turn out. We both have a desire to bring ourselves constantly into question and never be complacent.

— A mistake you would never want to make again? And, on the other hand, what do you think your greatest success has been?
Mistakes are even more important than successes. They are the lifeblood of a constantly evolving process. We believe that all mistakes should always be acknowledged—even in public, if necessary. We have had a number of important successes so far, but none of them has been quite like that of creating a gallery out of nothing, one that adopts a totally autonomous and original economic and cultural model.

— In practical terms, what does this autonomy and originality consist of?

At least the way we see it, its originality lies in the fact that we started with a frighteningly small budget, but we never once considered giving in to the attraction of the mainstream. On the contrary, we made a virtue of necessity, and we patiently started putting together a style that really does reflect our way of thinking—one that's based solely on our intuition and on the rapidity of our decisions. From an economic point of view, our enterprise has done really well, and it has taken shape totally autonomously, with no public funding. This means we have had no lack of difficulties, but it has given us a great sense of responsibility and pride.

— How is a young gallery like yours dealing with such a tough economic crisis?

Realism and prudence, coupled with an ability to resist difficulties and even find inspiration in them—this is what has helped us get through every crisis. However young it may be, our activity is healthy, it is constantly growing, and we intend to put on top-quality events by investing in research. The current crisis is not just economic but also social and behavioral, and it is seriously affecting the traditions of the art world. We have always been suspicious of consumerism and capitalism applied to art, and also of the greed and unscrupulousness of some of those who have taken advantage of a general lowering of the critical level. All this is now in crisis, and, we hope, it should clear the air and make way for strategies and attitudes based on greater respect and consensus.

— How would you advise a young collector just entering the world of contemporary art?

It depends on the young collector's degree of common sense and insight. Collecting doesn't mean buying objects to decorate your home with, nor does it mean buying them for short-term speculation. In times of crisis, collecting means sharing, not just owning. It means taking part with others to support an artist, and it means sharing the ideas and decisions of a gallery, and possibly even enjoying working on an ambitious project together.

— How do you mean? Are you thinking of involving the collector in creating a work or putting on an exhibition?

We've started involving some young collectors in the creation and production of works and projects. We try to encourage a sense of responsibility, focus, and awareness about the artistic operation as a form of interaction and dialogue, and not just as a market operation.

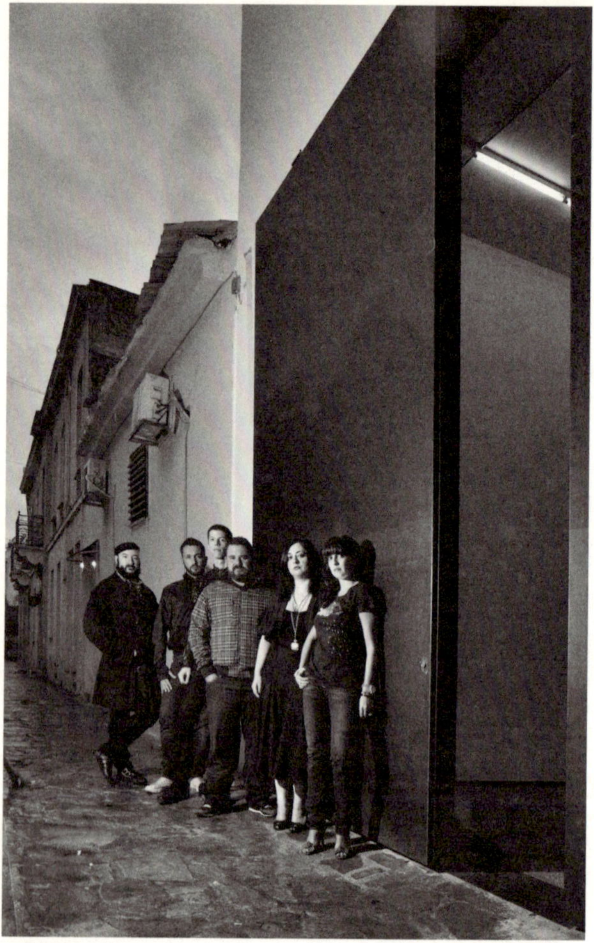

From left: George Vamvakidis, Dimitris Koulouris, Stephen Riolo, Stathis Panagoulis, Konstantina Soulioti, Nadia Gerazouni

Stathis Panagoulis and George Vamvakidis

THE BREEDER, ATHENS

— You opened your gallery in 2002, and within the space of a few years, you became the center of contemporary cultural life in Athens. What is your background story?

We met through a common friend in October 1999. At the time, we were living in different countries and really couldn't have been more different from each other, except that we were both interested in contemporary art, mainly through collecting. So we decided to enhance this common ground and commit to a relationship. *The Breeder* magazine was born not long afterward. Back then, *The Breeder* was a project magazine, more fun than real business, and it was mainly built on our relationship with the artists who were invited to participate, through projects made especially for us. *The Breeder* was based in Athens but would circulate globally. At some point, we used the spare space of the office premises for exhibitions of young Greek and foreign artists. Those shows became so popular and successful that it organically led us to turn *The Breeder* into a gallery.

— Last year you opened your new gallery in the Metaxourgeio district, and it was designed by Aris Zambicos. Why choose such a forceful architectural character when everyone else wants neutral spaces?
The architectural office 405 of Aris Zambicos proved able to realize the idiosyncratic ideas, obsessions, phobias, and aesthetic whims that possess us. Rather than a white cube, we went for a space with high character that closes in on the viewer, making the encounter with art more intense.

— How do you choose your artists? Do you have any particular advisers whom you trust?
We strongly believe that chemistry, ambition, and strong character should go hand in hand with great talent. All the artists we work with are first and foremost individuals we admire for their unique talents but also dear friends and colleagues. We trust the artists we already work with—who know well the profile and the goals of the gallery, and also our characters and tastes—to propose other artists or projects they think could be fitting for The Breeder profile. We like to do research through art schools and studio visits, but it is essential to spend time with an artist and get to know him or her before taking the next step. Lately, we have embarked on research into the older generation and historical Greek artists, some of whom—although greatly influential on the younger generation—seem to have been overlooked by the market.

— What sort of collecting do you work on? How much do you sell to Greek collectors, and how much to foreign ones?
From the start, we never solely relied on the local market. Nevertheless, Greek collectors who are very well informed and adventurous have always been supportive of us, although there were only a few when we first started in 2002. Since then, we have worked to cultivate a younger generation of collectors. Now that the market has expanded greatly in Athens, we work with a group of people who follow the gallery program but are also happy and excited to travel with us for new art discoveries.

— What are the greatest difficulties you find working in Athens?
Having a gallery in Athens has its advantages and disadvantages. For example, it may require double the effort to promote younger artists and get them out to an international context, but also we have the advantage and freedom to experiment more than, say, a gallery in New York. It's a pleasure to see the city change so rapidly, with more and more people becoming interested in contemporary art and in what we do. We also have to admit, though, that we always did things exactly the way we liked without complying to norms and rules.

— In recent years, the art scene in Athens has indeed grown and become extremely lively. What is behind this change?

The dynamic start of the Athens Biennial, the ReMap project in the center of Athens, a generation of young artists like Jannis Varelas, Athanasios Argianas, and Vangelis Vlahos, who are already showing internationally, and the hard work of some very active collectors, galleries, and curators. Athens has effectively entered the international art discourse.

— Is there something you can't stand about the job of a gallery owner?

The most painful thing about being a gallery owner is that more often than not you have to part with a great piece of art.

— Could you give some good advice to a young person who wants to open a gallery in Greece today?

There is plenty of room, and Athens is a strong and fast-developing market for contemporary art, so the more galleries there are, the better. Our advice would be: Just do it!

Toby Webster

THE MODERN INSTITUTE, GLASGOW

— Could you briefly tell me about the idea behind The Modern Institute? What inspired you to start?
The Modern Institute came about after I had worked at Transmission Gallery in Glasgow with Will Bradley. We both realized that there was a need for another organization that would work closely with artists, which is what we still like to do. We started by doing projects with artists who did not have representation elsewhere, and went on from there. The Modern Institute has been shaped over the past eleven years by the work we have done and the artists we represent. That was the idea—no idea, just do. I now work very closely with Andrew Hamilton, my director, and I also have a staff of about eight.

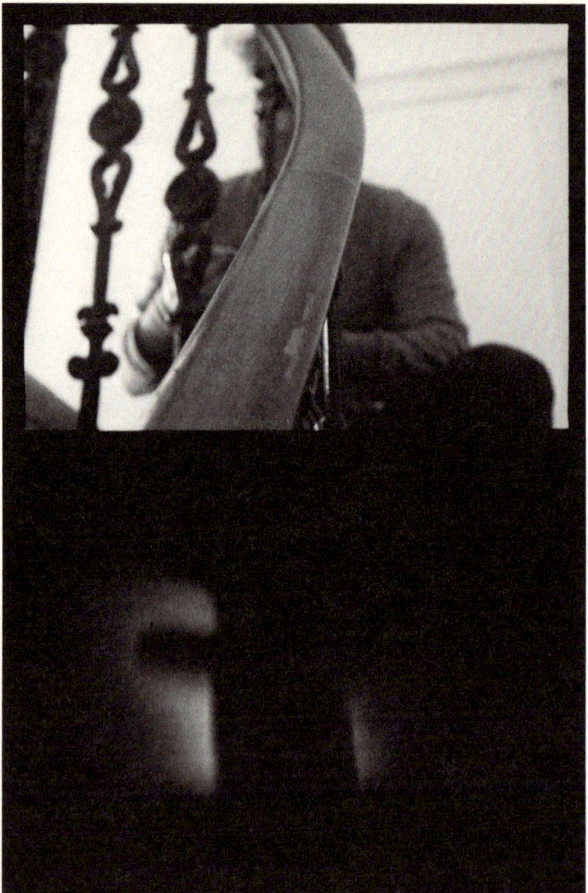

Toby Webster
Photo: Luke Fowler

— In the 1990s, you played a key role in bringing about the explosion of interest in contemporary art in Glasgow. What is your background?

I studied fine art at Glasgow School of Art. I had also studied architecture and design for a brief period before going to work for Ron Arad in London for a while.

— Who is the person who enabled you to become what you are today?

One thing about me is that I do not think of people as more or less important. They all have their roles in my life. I was always taught to appreciate everybody. People who think they are important tend to put me off. My father has always been a very exuberant person and my mother very creative, so they shaped my early experience . . . independence and confidence in my own thoughts made the rest.

— You've curated a number of historic exhibitions, including "Lovecraft" (1997), "Slipstream" (1998), and "My Head is on Fire but My Heart is Full of Love" (2002). In your opinion, what was your best curatorial project?

The one I love the most is "Strange I've Seen That Face Before," which was at the Museum Abteiberg in Germany in 2006. Director Susanne Titz was really amazing in giving me the chance to show works from the collection and add to it. My favorite room featured designer Christopher Dresser's toast racks, Andy Warhol wigs, Alessandro Mendini's "banal objects," and portraits by Andre Thomkins. This is a side of my practice I really love.

— Is there anything you can't stand about the job of a gallery owner?

Luckily, I love being a gallery owner.

— While chatting with Franco Noero and Gavin Brown at Art Basel in 2001, the three of you decided to open a gallery in Rome. Roma Roma Roma opened in June the following year, with a great exhibition featuring more than seventy artists. But the gallery closed a few years later. Why was that?

It had run its course as a project. All of our own individual galleries were starting to do very well, and because of the way we all run our galleries, which is really hands on, we found it just too much to continue. I must say it was a fantastic experience, and we really enjoyed being in Rome. And I loved the gallery—it was so different from Glasgow!

— Some important artists—like Simon Starling and Jim Lambie, to name just a couple—have come out of Glasgow. There isn't really much in the city aside from a few galleries, so what has made Glasgow so interesting for artists?

Glasgow has a great edge. It is challenging, and there are a great number of artists and people organizing events here. It's small enough to know what's happening but big enough not to get bored. And the quality of the shows is very high.

— Considering the increasing similarities between international exhibitions these days, what advice would you give to a young person who wants to become a curator?

I think that there are great curators. It's really important to work with artists to produce innovative and thought-provoking projects. Discussions with artists are the key to curating.

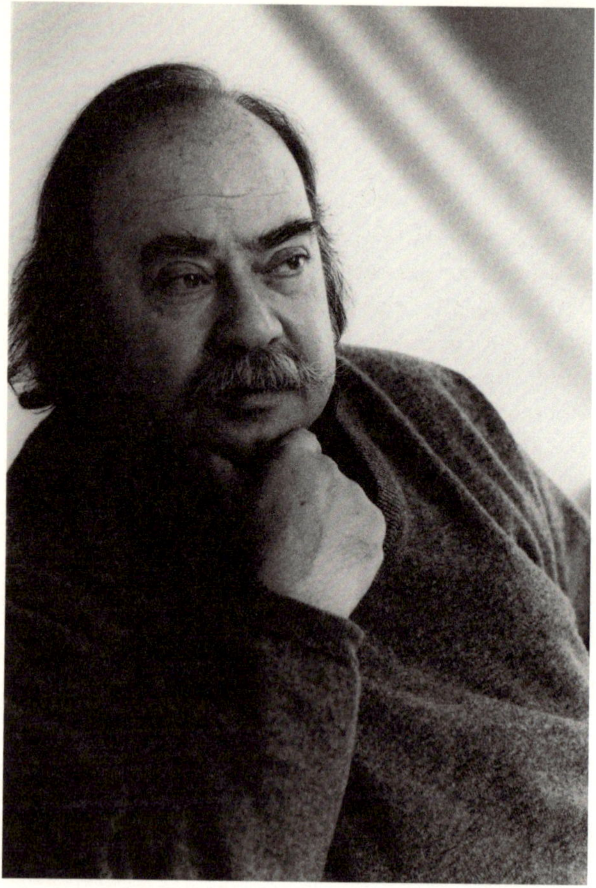

Antonio Tucci Russo
Photo: Nanda Lanfranco

Antonio Tucci Russo

TUCCI RUSSO STUDIO PER L'ARTE CONTEMPORANEA,

TORRE PELLICE

— You're a big name in the world of late twentieth-century art in Turin. When talking with Arte Povera artists, your name always comes up. And yet you were initially more interested in poetry and literature than in art. How and when did your adventure in the world of art begin?

I first came into contact with artists in 1963 and '64, when I was not only fairly actively involved in politics, but I was also especially interested in poetry. It happened with a group of poet friends: Gianni Milano, Vasco Are, and Paolo Cerrato, with whom I set up a little publishing company. It was directed by Are and was called Pitecantropus. The initiative was supported by Angelo Pezzana, a celebrated intellectual and the owner, in those days, of the Hellas bookshop in Turin. He also did the graphic design for our publications. These poems were accused of being obscene, and one of the defense witnesses during the court case that followed was Fernanda Pivano, whom I thus had the opportunity to meet. Other witnesses included friends, critics, intellectuals, and people from the theater—people such as Piero Gilardi, Giulio Carlo Argan, and Giordano Falzoni. Artists gave their spontaneous support for our case. It was the beginning of an adventure that led me to work with Gian Enzo Sperone as early as 1968, and I worked as his gallery director until 1974.

I should point out that those were years of the most extraordinary levels of visionary, international creativity, and it was possible to interact with artists on a daily basis, discussing their works and their upcoming exhibitions. It was a time of considerable intellectual development for me. I believe those were unique years, rich and exciting in terms of quality, and the result of a particular historical moment of great social change.

These events were also accompanied by great interest in culture as a whole, through underground cinema (New American Cinema and the Cooperativa del Cinema Indipendente Italiano) and experimental theater. There were people like Carmelo Bene, Leo de Berardinis, and Perla Peragallo, as well as the Living Theater, which was pretty well at home in Turin, together with poetry and literature. I also like to remember one wonderful evening we spent with Allen Ginsberg in Turin, with friends and artists. I'm mentioning all this to describe how the world of culture and the figurative arts were going through a period of extraordinary interaction.

— You were very young when you started working with Sperone. What were those years like? The photographer Paolo Mussat Sartor told me, for example, that you, Sperone, and practically all the Arte Povera artists used to meet every day at the gallery to discuss the works. Is that right?
Sperone and I used to meet a number of times during the week, and we would talk with the artists about projects for their new works while they were making them. After frequent travels around Europe and the United States, we would also talk to them about the new artists on the international scene and about exhibitions that the Sperone gallery might put on.

— Was there what you might call a "leader" in the Arte Povera group? Perhaps Michelangelo Pistoletto? Toward the mid-1960s, he was already working with prominent international galleries, while the other artists were only just starting to put on exhibitions in Italy. In your opinion, was Pistoletto somehow the group's mentor?
In those years, Pistoletto was certainly the artist who was best known by the public both in Italy and abroad for the all-encompassing nature of his creativity, including theater. I had the opportunity of working with him personally in 1966. It was for a show put on at the Piper in Turin, a magnificent discothèque designed and created by the architect

Piero Derossi. The title was *Cocapicco e Vestitorito*, and in the performance Michelangelo used a hundred meters of transparent plastic to make a bridal dress for Maria Pioppi, his companion in life and work. She was placed at the top of some wooden steps, at the foot of which a group of people created a city of sound and light, like a sort of little crib.

Even so, I would say the group never really had a leader, and this became apparent at Harald Szeemann's Documenta in 1972, where the individual art forms and personality of each artist became quite clear. Up until then, the movement had been united under the Arte Povera banner created by Germano Celant, but from then on each of the artists moved in a very personal direction.

— In 1967, Pistoletto announced opening his own studio to other artists. Poets Vasco Are and Gianni Milano, actor Carlo Colnaghi, and you took up the invitation to create your own works. Do you remember that day?

I remember that day very well because, as I was saying, Pistoletto and Pioppi were extraordinarily open to young people and new ideas, so lots of people used to go to Pistoletto's studio in 1966 and 1967. Among the various events was the first underground cinema in Turin, with Renato Ferraro, Franco Barberi,

Ugo Nespolo, Renato Dogliani, and others. And there was a poetry evening that Carlo Colnaghi came to. Colnaghi was a young street actor who had played a formative part in the Piccolo Teatro in Milan, and he worked with Pistoletto on all the theater projects. He then went on to be a film actor in a movie called *Manila Paloma Bianca*, directed by Daniele Segre, which received a mention at the Biennale Cinema in Venice. Renato Ferraro discovered Colnaghi in Milan, performing in a little play of his own, and he was invited to perform the same piece at the Chamber of Labor in Turin. Turin then became Colnaghi's adopted city. It was a very interesting evening, with lots of young people not only as spectators but also as professionals in other disciplines.

— In 1975, you and your wife Lisa decided to open a gallery of your own. How many collectors were there in Turin in those days? And how much of your audience came from outside the city?

Although Lisa and I were already together in 1975, she was only eighteen, and she didn't become part of the gallery until later, in 1982. In late 1974, I decided to open a gallery of my own and to start working on the Italian scene. Even though these artists had been presented by Sperone in previous years, they hadn't had the chance to fully express their potential in a world that was focused mainly on

American and European artists who, in those years, had important collectors like Panza di Biumo. The decision I made then was to highlight works of some of these Italian artists and to let them interact with the new situation that was emerging.
The first exhibition was of works by Pier Paolo Calzolari, and it was held in my first premises in Turin. This was in an old 250-square-meter garage in Via Calandra, where we displayed a series of works from 1966 to 1970, including a 1967 project that had originally been created for the Stedelijk Museum in Amsterdam but had never been realized. It consisted of an albino boxer flanked by pink polyhedrons made of ice that gradually melted.
The next exhibitions introduced a younger world, with Marco Bagnoli, Remo Salvatori, and later, in the new Corso Tassoni premises, which became the historic headquarters, Sandro Chia's first solo show. This was followed by Mario Merz, with whom I had the pleasure of working for a long time and whose studio was just next door to my gallery.
Turin has always been a city of idiosyncratic collectors. In those years, there was a small group of Turin-based and other Italian collectors who kept a close eye on the gallery's activities. I'd like to recall some of them: Corrado Levi, Guido Accornero, Giuseppe Panza di Biumo, Sandro Dorna, Marcello Levi, Angelo Baldassarre, and Franca and Marco Brignone. As for

foreign collectors, through Konrad Fischer, a great gallery owner and friend, I met Annick and Anton Herbert, who purchased two important exhibitions at my gallery.

— Over the years, you have watched the art world grow and, for better or worse, become what it is today. How do you view this transformation?
The art world grew in terms of information. In the 1980s, the first public institutions started appearing in Italy, which for years had survived on only the work of private galleries. Over the years, this growth, which was useful for spreading information, gave the market a level of importance that was too great, creating an imbalance between quality and mere production. What I don't like about the present system is the fact that many young galleries are following more in the footsteps of those that have acquired economic power over the market than those that have carried out research into the history of contemporary art. There are plenty of examples . . .

— In the early 1990s, you and Lisa made a radical decision: You closed the gallery in Turin and opened another one in Torre Pellice, a little town at the foot of the mountains, an hour's drive away from the city. Why was that? Weren't you afraid of being too isolated?

The 1980s and '90s brought about a whole series of significant changes in the art market and art world. The return of painting gave new impetus to the market, which also received support from institutions—especially those abroad—and the area of art that used more complex creative languages and made fewer concessions to the image found itself in crisis. The 1990s brought the Gulf War, and this led to international shockwaves that weakened national economies and led to a consequent crisis in the art system, which for many years found itself in an unfavorable economic position.

Lisa and I thought that Turin couldn't offer the right degree of energy at that time, because it was embroiled in serious social problems, and this meant that culture had great difficulty creating its own space for survival. This led to our departure from the city, and we entered the more neutral and, at the same time, more real world of Torre Pellice, a little town up against the mountains with a Protestant minority that, over the years, has defended its own identity and culture. We found a late nineteenth-century factory building and decided to move in, bringing our own history with us, while continuing research and dialogue with the older and younger generations. The fact that the gallery was some way from the city meant that those who came were really interested. We made some carefully targeted changes: staying open on

Sundays, longer exhibitions that last at least three months, and a number of shows on at the same time. We never thought of isolating ourselves or snubbing the city. On the contrary, we wanted to open up the area and make it a hub where things could happen.

— What do you think a gallery owner's role should be?
I think that a gallery owner, if he or she wants to remain one, should always keep in mind his or her relationships with the artists. You need to keep your awareness and knowledge of what the artists are doing very much alive, and never let yourself be drawn into futile competition with other galleries. It's important to know how to manage exhibitions not just in economic terms, but first and foremost in terms of informing the public and using the instruments that the system offers you. This is a job that requires various levels of contact, from personal interaction with the collectors closest to the gallery, to participation in national and international fairs, to managing contacts with the institutions, and so on.

— And what is the role of art?
The role of art is to maintain its own power and its own mystery without either being lost over time.

— Many people think the current economic crisis will be beneficial for art. Do you agree?

During economic crises, one has more time to think about the individual roles of those who work in the art world, and one needs to go back to and improve particular areas of expertise. This normally improves both the market, which gets a greater grip on reality, and the work itself.

— How do you see the future of your extraordinary gallery in Torre Pellice? It is perhaps one of the loveliest and most appealing private spaces in Europe.
Thank you. We believe that a gallery should end its time only when the art itself forces it to, not the market. So long as the artists are by our side, we shall be with them.

Jarrod Rawlins

UPLANDS, PRAHRAN VICTORIA

— You opened your first gallery with Blair Trethowan in Melbourne's Chinatown in 2001. You had both just finished your art studies. It was a little claustrophobic place next to a sex shop, but it immediately became a center for the city's art scene. What made your place so special?

It was generational and class-based. Most existing gallery owners were middle-aged women with galleries propped up by wealthy families or husbands. We were a couple of Westies with no money, putting ourselves in the same context. People found that interesting, I guess. We were also the first to exhibit contemporary art that had concerns outside decoration, something that had a theoretical or social concern. So many of the galleries who presented themselves as exhibiting contemporary art had previously shown really bad artists like Brett Whiteley or Howard Arkley—just total rubbish. So it was refreshing for a lot of people to come into our crappy little gallery and see installations and videos—you know, normal art, not exhibition after exhibition of banal, parochial Australian painting or some quasi-avant-garde crap or poetic video rubbish.

So I guess that's what made our place special: It was actually representative of something that we felt was taking place all over the world. It felt like it was alive.

— How did you choose your artists? How did you devise your program, and what, in your opinion, were the most interesting projects in those years?
There are so many ways and reasons for choosing to work with an artist, and over the years I have never really worked out a clear answer. One thing that was super important to us was that the artist had to be active within the art community. We wanted to work with people whose practice extended outside their studios. That may have taken the form of curating shows, being on boards of artist-run spaces, publishing, teaching, writing, collaboration—you get the picture. We have never really been that interested in artists who isolate themselves in some romantic idea of what constitutes creativity.
The program was pretty organic when we started. Now I like to have the program locked in twelve to eighteen months in advance, but back then it was only a couple of months in advance, and even that could change easily. Everyone had more energy for what we were doing back then. Now that everyone is older, things move more slowly. We have always wanted the program to be broken up so that shows/artists with too much in common were not

close together. We also included more project shows back at the start—by that I mean working with artists that we didn't represent, different galleries, groups, etc. So there was never really any plan to the program, it was totally organic—beer and cigarettes in the stairwell, making decisions when we were drunk, that kind of thing. The most interesting projects back then were the ones that had no plan, which was pretty much all of them. We thought we had plans, thought we were organized, but we weren't. The most interesting projects for me were attending the art fairs, Artissima and Frieze. That was really great fun, trying to work out how to do it; not having any expectations made it so much easier. Meeting other galleries doing the same thing as us was great, it reinforced what we were doing in Melbourne.

— After Blair's tragic death in 2006, rumor had it that the gallery was going to close. But your wife, Tara, decided to join in, and you moved to larger premises, where the gallery embarked on a new life. How did people react to this change? And how did the gallery's activities change?
I don't really recall how people reacted to the change, to be honest. I do remember that after Blair's death, I decided I really didn't care about other people's opinions, especially people in the art world, so I don't know what they thought. At a time like that, everyone

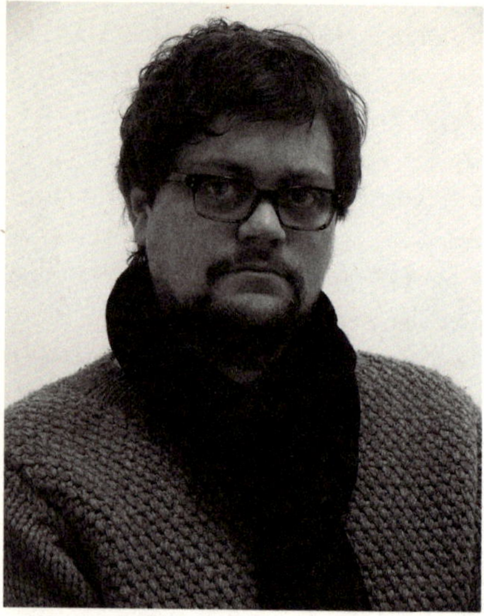

Jarrod Rawlins

is very polite because they are scared of upsetting you, so you could never really tell what people thought about the change. The move changed the way many artists approached the space. It made some people produce larger objects. Some artists struggled with the change of space, and for some it was really successful. We have also taken on many more artists in the past couple of years, and that has been the biggest change. The funny thing is that we recently moved again to a smaller space. I like it better than the bigger one.

— What percentage of your sales take place at art fairs? How many fairs do you go to outside Australia? And how are you coping with the crisis?
We originally aimed to attend one fair per year outside Australia, but the reality is we haven't. We will probably start that again next year, but we have spent money moving and preparing the new space recently so that was enough this year. And 2009 has been quiet, so it's a nice year to have off. The percentage of our sales from fairs is low, but I don't know the exact number. I think that is the case with most Australian galleries attending American and European fairs—if they say otherwise, I think they are probably talking themselves up. But we get a good amount of follow-up from attending fairs, that is the main reason we attend, it's super important exposure. You ask the European art world to name Australian dealer galleries, and they will say Uplands and Roslyn Oxley; the rest are invisible.
As for the crisis right now, things are bad. The smart collectors are getting access to great works right now, and they are getting good discounts. I wish I was buying more.

— What do you think your best instinct has been, and what mistake will you be careful not to make again?
I thought that in mid-2007 the market felt like it was going to collapse, so I think the best instinct

I have had was to stop attending fairs for 2008–2009 and to reduce overheads by moving the gallery by 2009. I have done both, and it seems to be working, so I am happy with that. But really the best intuition I had was to open in the first place. No regrettable mistakes.

— What do you think the Australian art system is in need of, and what are its most interesting aspects?
The Australian art system is in need of some belief in itself. It needs more collectors who are willing to take proper risks, not faux risks. Buying a good video work is not a fucking risk. Investing in something that has no visible return is a risk, supporting something without receiving a tax break is a risk. The system here is still so young, some thirty to forty years old. There is no real history of collecting, no history of philanthropy—we need to learn the value of that. I think the most interesting aspect of the Australian system is our ability to send craft and parochialism to Venice. It's overwhelming, I mean I don't think it's good at all, it's crap, but it is a super interesting thing to observe. Time after time we send the same predictable shit. That is what we are in need of, confidence—there's no confidence here.

— Do galleries and museums in Australia cooperate and work together?

You would like to think so, but I don't really think they do. It depends on the museum and gallery. If the gallery is linked to a high-powered source of wealth, then the museums will work extremely well with them. The museums in Australia are always crying poor—I don't know, perhaps they are, perhaps they just have too many wages to pay. So if the museum can get the gallery to assist with funding aspects of an exhibition like freight, publishing, and son on, then there is cooperation. Generally, there is still a very old-fashioned understanding of what a museum is in Australia. Most of the state museums haven't worked out how to work closely with the galleries, how that could be of advantage to everyone. They just like having board meetings and cups of tea.

— How do you imagine your future? And what would you have liked to do if you hadn't become a gallery owner?

My future is totally unknown and probably unpredictable. I can see myself surviving this recession, just, and coming out the other side with a great group of artists and collectors to work with. The gallery will expand but not become too wanky with two spaces and anachronistic presentation approaches like that. I would like to remain totally hands-on in this business. I don't want hordes of gallerinas, that kind of bullshit. It is important to stay as close as you can to what you do, otherwise you might as well sell B&B Italia furniture or used sports cars. I am also interested in continuing with my academic life. I will probably begin a book on the history of twentieth-century Australian art soon, that will be fun. If I hadn't become a gallery owner, I think I would have liked to be a mountaineer, a Sherpa perhaps.

Zhang Wei

VITAMIN CREATIVE SPACE, GUANGZHOU, BEIJING

— Vitamin is considered one of China's top galleries. You are highly appreciated as a curator, and you have considerable international experience. What is your background? Where did you study, and how did you first enter the art world?

I studied English at college in China, and later on I received a master's in creative curating at Goldsmiths in London. It was really by chance that I started to love art. After I graduated from college, I was looking for a job, and I heard that Dutch curator Hans Van Dijk needed an assistant in his research of Chinese contemporary art, and that's how I got involved.

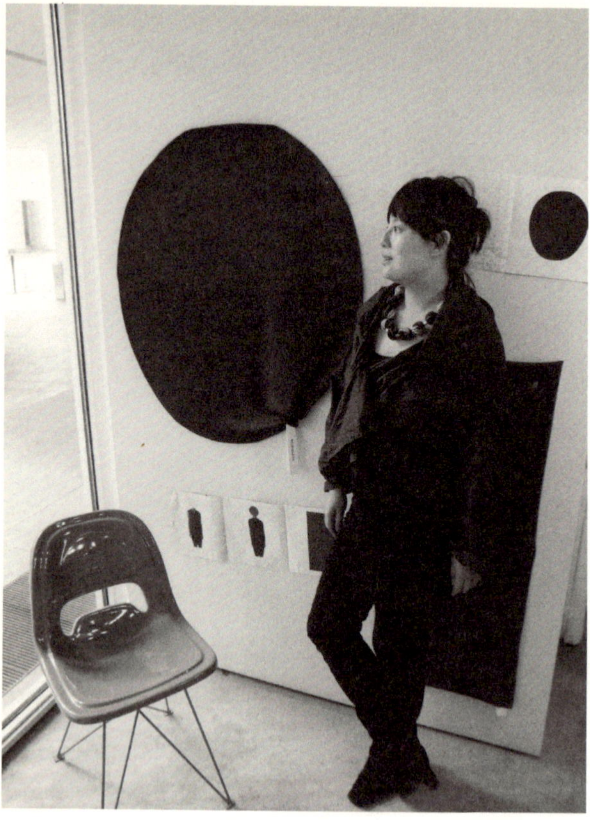

Zhang Wei

— Vitamin is a commercial gallery that acts like a nonprofit institution. You put on workshops, conferences, symposiums, and more. When I interviewed you in Beijing some years ago for *Flash Art*, you said, "The essential objective of Vitamin is to understand what contemporary art in China is, and what contemporary art can mean or accomplish in the Chinese context." So now I'll ask you: What is Chinese art, and what can art mean in China today?

After so many years' work, I have to say there is no "Chinese art," there is just "art in China." Even as an institution, or an agent of art, what you care about is not solely the art; you also care about the system that art lives and flows in. The art scene in China is very different from that of other places. As an art space, we need to respond to the creativity of artists in Chinese contexts.

— You opened Vitamin in 2002, and the speed with which it gained international recognition is pretty impressive. You're very careful about how you present yourself abroad: Your first public appearances in Europe occurred when you were opening your premises in Guangzhou. Is that right? Do you consider a sense of strategy and communication to be one of your talents?

I am not sure that we have the same understanding about strategy, but I do think there is an awareness involved in the process of developing Vitamin Creative Space. I mentioned understanding the significance of building up a space in China. It's not just a matter of building up a physical space but of forming an invisible social space that keeps on communicating with the artist's creativity. It's a long-term process, and it needs a kind of philosophical approach.

— The growth of the art system in China has been extremely rapid. Within the space of fifteen years, Chinese contemporary art went from being totally ignored to an authentic phenomenon. In the past seven or eight years, many galleries in the West have started hunting for Chinese artists as if they were on a big-game safari in Africa. Do think the present financial crisis might help the Chinese art system to slow down a bit and take a healthy pause?
I'm not sure there really is an "art system" in China. For the past few years, what I see is a rapid growth of interest in the Chinese art market. The booming art scene was built up mainly with this in mind. But we can all see that an art "system" is highly complex, with many layers. I think the crisis makes people here aware of that.

— Have you been affected by the crisis? What has changed or will change in your way of working?
I think the crisis will affect everybody in one way or

another, so Vitamin is no exception. But there's good and bad in everything. You might lose something in the market, but you might have more to gain by thinking about the super-important things. Art is different from commercial commodities; it's not just about the market. It has something more than that, which was lost when the market was booming. Now I think this "something" is coming back, which is good.

— Why do you think Chinese collectors have such little interest in Western art?
Any serious interest in art needs time, otherwise it just becomes a bubble! That's what I would like to believe about your question.

— What advice would you give to a young collector interested in Chinese art?
Be passionate about it. Remain curious not just about Chinese art but about all Chinese culture. Never stop challenging yourself.

Jocelyn Wolff

GALERIE JOCELYN WOLFF, PARIS

— I remember that a few years ago, when everyone was making a hullabaloo about the new Leipzig "school" of painting, you too were taking an interest in the non-painting side of the city's art scene. This rather struck me as a sign of your independence. I imagine your interest came from your friendship with Alexander Koch, an assistant at the local fine arts school. Where did you meet Alexander, and how did he influence the program of your Paris gallery?

I met Alexander through his wife, artist Valérie Favre. While working as an assistant at Crédac, the contemporary art center in Ivry, in 1995, I helped Valérie put up a large video and painting installation,

Les restes de la Méduse (The Remainders of the Medusa). Not long afterward, Valérie and I met again when I was working as a publisher, and one issue of my contemporary art magazine *Ninety* was dedicated to her work. It was a couple years later in Berlin that Valérie introduced me to Alexander. At the time, he was an assistant at the Hochschule für Grafik und Buchkunst in Leipzig, in the class of Astrid Klein, and a curator who had put on some striking shows.

I recall well how, for the very first time, I was able to really discuss art with someone, and even agree on a few points. I have a very strong *esprit de contradiction*, and it is very rare for me to find people who are not bored, ruffled, or disturbed by my way of discussing things passionately and intensely. Alexander gave me the chance to meet with artists while they were still studying. Among them, there were some painters who did become famous later on. I knew then that they would be successful, I mean, from a market perspective, but I felt that this art was not for me. It was too far from what really interested me and still interests me today. My feeling was that the Conceptual scene in Leipzig, although very dense and rich, was largely ignored (and perhaps still is). This idea of a "scene" is something that did not really exist in France—although this may not be the place to engage in this debate—and I was troubled by the fact that it was very difficult for painters from France to emerge, regardless of their artistic qualities. For me, starting a gallery meant wanting to make particular, deserving artistic positions visible in the art field; it did not mean recuperating work done by others elsewhere.

— You're French and your gallery is in Paris, but most of your artists are German. How would you characterize their art? What is it in German art that excites you?
I do view the art scene in Germany as being richer, denser, and more complex than elsewhere in the world. I am convinced that there is practically no one who is a real expert on this scene as a whole: You have the Hamburg scene, and those of the great art schools in Karlsruhe, Leipzig, Munich, Berlin, and so on. There is no "German art," per se. There is a multiplicity of schools, cities, scenes, generations, with multiple and paradoxical traditions.
One needs to keep in mind that the debate regarding contemporary art is more rooted in a historical and political consciousness in Germany than anywhere else. Documenta has this same origin: an absolute, existential need to pursue cultural production, while integrating both the failure of Western civilization and its fantastic cultural past. When it comes to culture, there is a need to prolong the tradition (in its Latin sense, *traditio*), would you not agree? The German art

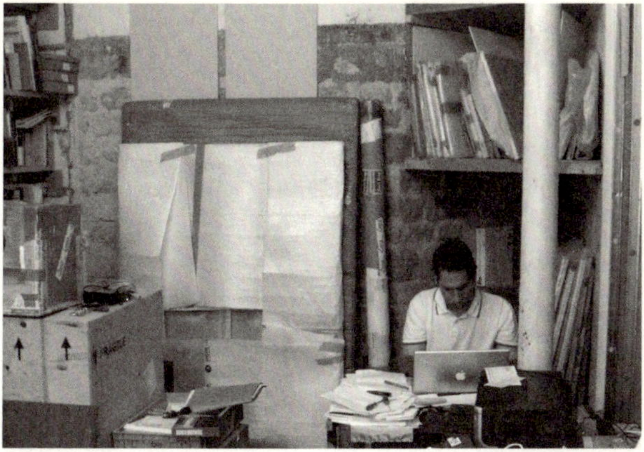

Jocelyn Wolff

scene was also nourished by a strong connection to the United States, as can be seen in the case of Black Mountain College.

There is no “German art,” because you have such a variety of practices: the curatorially correct school of neo-conceptualism that found a large audience, the Reactionary school (that had some good figures too, I must admit: Chateaubriand was a Reactionary and still is an important writer), the “Socio-kitsch School” (artists creating stuff to illustrate social issues that found an audience of attentive curators), and “export art,” created for the American market . . .

In Germany, I find art which is formally strong but also rooted in this historical and political consciousness, and this is what interests me. I can find this elsewhere as well—and I have.
Why so many German artists have became fashionable and visible is a parallel debate: it is more a question of how "hype coefficients" are constructed to establish artists. Each artist has a certain coefficient of hype, determined by the network promoting his work, his attitude, discourse, etc. How does it work and who are the actors of this system? I could undertake to answer these questions but it would quickly become controversial. To answer why such a system functions is not so easy: of course, we would need to evoke the presence of money and power backing some specific interest, yet we'd also need to discuss the absence of memory, the lack of critical discourse.

— So what is your background? As far as I know, you studied philosophy. Is that right?
I studied political science, political philosophy, and art in Strasbourg and Paris. I never finished my Ph.D because I found a stimulating job in an art magazines publishing company and did not manage to do both.

— Your gallery opened in 2003, so it's still pretty young. How does a young gallery owner manage to work with talented artists without them being snatched

away by more powerful galleries? In your case, for example, I'm thinking of Clemens von Wedemeyer, an artist whom you presented at Art Statements at Art Basel and who took part in Skulptur Projekte Münster in 2007. Or Guillaume Leblon, who is developing an international career.

I really had to fight so that the gallery would not be seen as a "fish pond" where big galleries could catch emerging artists just at the precise moment they gained international visibility. How? By obtaining very high results from the gallery's promotional work, a kind of work that is very difficult to obtain even for a powerful gallery that works with many more artists, but with less passion and less expertise. Yet the gallery had to learn fast. We engaged in wonderful partnerships with other galleries, both young (such as ProjecteSD, in Barcelona) and well-established (such as Nächst St. Stephan, in Vienna). We also focused on placing works in major collections right away, because we knew without a doubt that our gallery artists were at that level.

— What advice could you offer a young collector who is just now starting to look at contemporary art.

Ooof! It is difficult to give any kind of "general" advice. For me, each person deserves individual advice. People have very different approaches to art: Some are too impulsive, some too shy, superficial or fundamentalist, etc. It depends on the person.

— After a long period of isolation, Paris is once again becoming an important center for contemporary art. How you find working in this city? Do you feel you have the support of its collectors and its art system?
I love living and working here. Paris is a very open city for art. It is not provincial and is no longer arrogant. The collectors do support us, but one has to work internationally, anyhow. We also have strong ties with French institutions: I often see curators and museum directors in the gallery. In Paris, we are very fortunate to make artistic positions visible to an audience that is both receptive and diverse. The quality of the shows is always a priority. There is always so much to see in the city, and we are located in Belleville—an emerging neighborhood that is still clearly off the beaten path. We compensate for this fragile aspect with stronger shows.

— On the subject of exhibitions, could you tell me which ones you're proudest of, and why?
I guess the first solo exhibition by Katinka Bock, "*Bäume wachsen und Ströme fliessen: Wasser, Wärme, Monument*" (Trees Grow and Fluids Flow: Water, Heat, Monument, 2007) as well as all exhibitions by Guillaume Leblon. These are two artists whose practices are linked to exhibition making. In their shows, the relationship with the context of the gallery was very strong—the gallery as a space, as a place with a

certain history, in a certain neighborhood. Christoph Weber also made a fantastic project here dealing with the history of the Paris Commune: The very last barricade was fifty meters away from the gallery.

— What's your strategy for dealing with the financial crisis?

A few classic recipes: low fixed costs, affordable prices for emerging artists, strong historical positions with fair prices, no return to a regional/national basis (I am not planning to show small drawings and consider art collectors as philatelists). Only a cutting-edge program can lift us above reactionary attempts. I really believe that art (not only contemporary) should not be exaggeratedly expensive; good pricing is a major issue. But this has to be thought of before difficulties arise: It is very difficult to fix mistakes made in the past.

— Jocelyn, you give the impression of being a serious sort, someone who doesn't laugh much. Is that correct?

Oh yes, I am quite a serious and boring person.

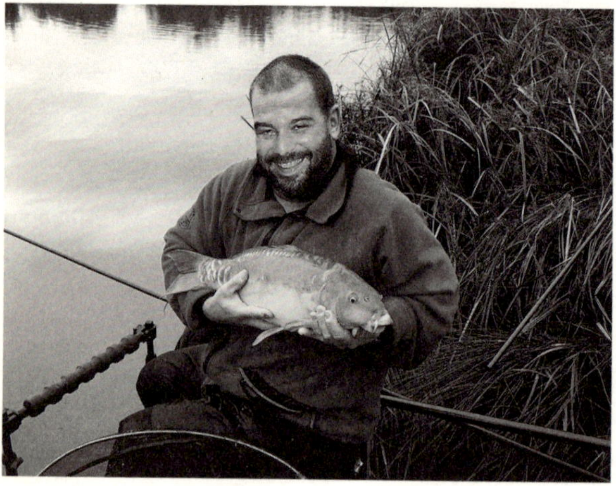

Paolo Zani

Paolo Zani

GALLERIA ZERO..., MILAN

— Like some other Italian gallery owners, such as Massimo De Carlo and Franco Noero, you don't have an art-history education. What is your background? How did start working in art?

I was studying at the Faculty of Medicine in Parma. In 1992, I stumbled across contemporary art by chance. I was a stretcher-bearer at the hospital, and in those days, I used to go twice a week to Massimo De Carlo's gallery in Milan, on Via Bocconi, where I worked on the installation and storage of works. In 1998, I became part of the official staff and started working with Uwe Schwarzer on the logistics for the new premises on Viale Corsica.

— I imagine that apprenticeship was quite an experience. What did you learn from Massimo?

It was an important opportunity for me, and I was lucky to walk into the gallery one day as a small collector and come out as an assistant. He was always very generous with his opinions when I had some question to ask him—I really do thank him. I'm very fond of Massimo.

— You opened your first gallery in Piacenza in 2000. Why there? Did you not feel sure enough to open one in a more important city?
I didn't feel the slightest bit sure the gallery would survive. It was a preparatory step, a sort of workshop to figure things out. The fact that my expenses were lower than they would have been in Milan was an important factor in my decision. I didn't have any collectors, so it was certainly a rash thing to do.

— Did your move to Milan bring more business?
The three previous years in Piacenza, from 2000 to 2003, had given me the time and opportunity to realize how dramatic the situation really was. The move to Milan also brought expansion in economic terms—in Piacenza I'd sold two works to two people in the town in three years. However, I did have some support from a few collectors outside Piacenza, whom I had met during my previous experience.

— How do you choose your artists? Whom do you trust?
I trust in my own obsessions and visions. I am always hoping that a revelation, an epiphany, will suddenly materialize before me.

— What is the best strategy for buying? Should you haggle?
Bargaining = cholinergic urticaria. It gives you a rash.

— What can you not stand in a collector? What should they never do when buying a work?
It's hard for me to keep calm when someone asks me if a work will be a good investment.

— You're one of the youngest gallery owners I've interviewed for this book. What advice do you have for a collector your own age who is just starting to buy art in this period of recession?
First of all, I'm convinced that young collectors are actually quite lucky to be starting out at a time like this, a rather precarious period, as it allows them to cultivate their passion with greater intensity. They should be able to achieve their objective—creating a top-quality collection—probably with a smaller economic outlay, and with the advantage of being able to obtain more important works more easily. However, they shouldn't think of art as a form of speculation; if they do, it quite simply won't work.

— What do you think your greatest success has been? And your greatest mistake?
My greatest success is yet to come, of course. The worst mistake I made was in July 1970: I was going like a rocket and didn't even realize.

— Are you afraid of the future?
Being afraid of the future isn't one of my obsessions.

That's one less—and a good thing too. I must say I find it rather narrow minded, at least in terms of defending one's own personal interests and one's own plot of land. I really do think that metaphysical, revelatory, epiphanic encounters can happen at any time. They're unexpected by definition. And then a passion for and love of our species—with its total inability to accept its own condition, and the aesthetic dimension that this condition tends to create—is central to my vision of the future.

— What is the future of your gallery? Is there a model that you aspire to?
Recently, entropy has been pretty mischievous with regard to our project. I want to live this moment intensely. The future of the gallery is fundamentally based on building a history that, by definition, is currently being defined. I dreamed of Lars Von Trier's latest film—the one that will never come out. It's called *Lilian*. I spoke to Christian about it.

— What do you think a gallery owner should never reveal to a collector?
What an artist might say about him . . .

— Gino De Dominicis, great snob that he was, liked to maintain that there is no art world, there is only art in the world. What is your view?

My vision of art is vaguely martial. Stripped, however, of that ecumenical aura that characterized a political moment and a particular stance adopted by society (I'm referring to the 1970s). An attitude that was however fundamentally "cool" and sustainable, and that in the end meant that it couldn't keep its commitments to society.

These days, that sort of approach finds much less fertile ground, so it's harder to maintain. I'm still referring to what is basically a political role of the artist and gallery owner. But not in the way our predecessors expected. I think that, as always, there are huge problems of comprehension between the generations, with our fathers expecting something from us that we neither can nor want to give. I believe the provocative gesture needs to be accompanied by abdication.

And I also think that the value of a work of art is actually directly proportional to the degree of anti-entropy it expresses. But, since I'm not such as snob, I believe that even a good hyper-entropic work can admirably represent our imperfection and our infinite need for consolation.

Series' Editor
LIONEL BOVIER

Author
ANDREA BELLINI

Editorial Coordination
NICOLETTA ESPOSITO
HARULA PEIROLO

Editing and Proofreading
NIKKI COLUMBUS
GEOFF LOWE
LAURA TRAVERSI
SIMON TURNER

Translations
LUCA ANDRIOLO
LOREDANA BAROZZINO
LAURA TRAVERSI
SIMON TURNER

Design
CHIARA FIGONE

Typeface
HERMES-SANS (WWW.OPTIMO.CH)

Cover
MAURIZIO CATTELAN,
A Perfect Day, 1999
Courtesy
Galleria Massimo de Carlo, Milano

Print
MUSUMECI S.P.A.,
Quart (Aosta)

Partner for the publication

nationale suisse

Printed in Europe

Published by
JRP|Ringier
Letzigraben 134
CH-8047 Zurich
Tel +41 (0) 43 311 27 50
Fax +41 (0) 43 311 27 51
www.jrp-ringier.com
info@jrp-ringier.com

ISBN 978-3-03764-087-6

Also available: Italian edition,
ISBN 978-3-03764-088-3

JRP|Ringier books are available internationally at selected bookstores and from the following distribution partners:

SWITZERLAND
Buch 2000, AVA Verlagsauslieferung AG, Centralweg 16, CH-8910 Affoltern a.A., buch2000@ava.ch, www.ava.ch

FRANCE
Les Presses du réel, 35 rue Colson, F-21000 Dijon, info@lespressesdureel.com, www.lespressesdureel.com

GERMANY AND AUSTRIA
Vice Versa Vertrieb, Immanuelkirchstrasse 12, D-10405 Berlin, info@vice-versa-vertrieb.de, www.vice-versa-vertrieb.de

UK AND OTHER EUROPEAN COUNTRIES
Cornerhouse Publications, 70 Oxford Street, UK-Manchester M1 5NH, publications@cornerhouse.org, www.cornerhouse.org/books

USA, CANADA, ASIA, AND AUSTRALIA
D.A.P./Distributed Art Publishers, 155 Sixth Avenue, 2nd Floor, USA-New York, NY 10013, dap@dapinc.com, www.artbook.com

For a list of our partner bookshops or for any general questions, please contact JRP|Ringier directly at info@jrp-ringier.com, or visit our homepage www.jrp-ringier.com for further information about our program.

In the same series

Andrea Bellini (ed.)
Collecting Contemporary Art
ISBN 978-3-03764-015-9

Malcolm McLaren (ed.)
Musical Paintings
ISBN 978-3-03764-058-6